SCREEN SAVED

PERIL AND PROMISE OF MEDIA IN MINISTRY

Dan Andriacco

ST. ANTHONY MESSENGER PRESS

Cincinnati, Ohio

for ANN, *with love*

Scripture citations are taken from the *New Revised Standard Version Bible*, copyright ©1989 by the Division of Christian Education of the National Council of Churches of Christ in the U.S.A. and used by permission.

Excerpts from Michael Crichton's *Timeline*, copyright ©1999, and *Airframe*, copyright ©1996, used by permission of Alfred A. Knopf, a division of Random House, Inc.

Excerpt from Thomas Merton's *New Seeds of Contemplation*, copyright ©1961 by the Abbey of Gethsemani, Inc., used by permission of New Directions Publishing, and the Trustees of the Merton Legacy Trust.

Cover design by Constance Wolfer
Interior design by Sandy L. Digman
Electronic format and pagination by Sandy L. Digman

ISBN 0-86716-418-2
Copyright ©2000 by Dan Andriacco

Published by St. Anthony Messenger Press
www.AmericanCatholic.org

Printed in the U.S.A.

CONTENTS

Acknowledgments

This book is the outgrowth of a long and still continuing journey. I've had many guides along the way. Thanks are in order.

First I must thank those who made this book and all that I do possible:

My Wife, ANN BRAUER ANDRIACCO, and our three most successful mutual projects—DANIEL, MICHAEL AND ELIZABETH ANDRIACCO. They put up with a lot.

Thanks also to the following for other important contributions:

MOM AND DAD, for giving me life and so much more, and my big brother, Tony, for letting me live despite extreme provocation;

MARIANNE E. ROCHE, ESQ., lawyer and mystic, who doesn't own a television set and yet manages to remain plugged in to popular culture. She pointed me in the right direction;

THE MOST REV. DANIEL E. PILARCZYK, Archbishop of Cincinnati; the REV. CHRISTOPHER R. ARMSTRONG, Chancellor of the Roman Catholic Archdiocese of Cincinnati; and the late REV. RICHARD MARZHEUSER, former dean of Mount St. Mary's Seminary, each of whom read and critiqued the draft of my doctoral dissertation that was the basis of chapters one through three;

REVS. DEL STAIGERS and JEFF KEMPER, of the Athenaeum of Ohio/Mount St. Mary's Seminary, who read and commented upon sections of the dissertation relevant to their specialties;

Professors RICK DIETRICH and JAMES HUDNUT-BEUMLER, my examining committee at Columbia Theological Seminary, who nursed my doctoral dissertation through to completion (with Rick making brilliant suggestions for sharpening the text);

All of my wonderful TEACHERS and FELLOW STUDENTS—too many to name—at the Athenaeum of Ohio/Mount St. Mary's Seminary, the University of Dayton, and Columbia Theological Seminary, whose insights have influenced every page of this work and made it possible;

All of the AUTHORS QUOTED HEREIN, on whose shoulders I stand. In particular, I gratefully acknowledge the key work of NEIL POSTMAN. He asked in print the question that I had to answer in order to know how to do ministry in a media age.

Introduction

A Catholic priest or deacon has about ten minutes a week to reach with his homily the most faithful members of his flock, those who attend Mass every Sunday. A Protestant minister may preach as much as twenty or thirty minutes. But television never stops preaching and teaching, and the average American tunes in more than four hours a day.

That's the reason for this book.

For nearly twenty-four years I was a member of the media, first as a reporter and then as business editor for a daily newspaper. I had no intention of abandoning that career when I began theological studies at the Athenaeum of Ohio/Mount St. Mary's Seminary in Cincinnati. I returned to the classroom as a first step toward seeking ordination as a deacon. But by the time I received my Master of Arts in Religion from the Athenaeum, I had discerned a call to a different ministry.

Toward the end of my time as a student at the Athenaeum, I became fascinated with the tension between the mass media by which I was surrounded (and was part of) and the gospel in which I believed. In an independent study with Father David DeVore at the Athenaeum and several classes at the University of Dayton's Institute for Pastoral Communications (now the Institute for Pastoral Initiatives), I began exploring such questions as: What values messages do the mass media send in our culture? How do they compare to the values of the gospel? How do these media—in form as well as content—affect the way people think about religion, God and church? How can Christian believers use the technology and the stories of the culture to proclaim Christ?

When I told a close friend and seminary classmate about this growing interest, she said, "That doesn't sound like a deacon."

Eventually the Holy Spirit convinced me that she was right. Instead of applying to enter the deacon formation program, I continued my exploration of mass media and the gospel at Columbia Theological Seminary near Atlanta. The "Gospel and Culture" track of Columbia's Doctor of Ministry program gave me a structure and a community to pursue my thinking and research, taking me in directions I had never dreamed of when my journey began. I wrote articles for numerous religious publications, taught courses on "Media and Moral Values" at the College of Mount St. Joseph in Cincinnati and "Ministry for a Media Age" at the Athenaeum and even switched careers: I became the director of the Office of Communications for the Archdiocese of Cincinnati—a job ideally suited to my professional training and my interests.

In reading and annotating almost 150 books and articles, I never found one that provided in one place everything a pastoral minister needs to minister in a media age: an understanding of how the culture industries work, a spiritual framework for relating to mass media, tools for reading the "signs of the times" in media and comparing/contrasting them to the gospel, and practical guidance on rejecting, challenging or using media in specific contexts in a ministry setting.

That's What This Book Does

This is a handbook for all ministers of the church—priests, pastoral associates, directors of religious education, catechists, youth ministers, Catholic school and parish school of religion teachers and chaplains. If you're active in a ministry, whether paid or volunteer, this book is for you. For, whatever your charism, you need to understand how media affect your ministry and how you can use media to make your ministry more effective. This book will help.

The first three chapters look at the media environment in

which we live and minister. Chapter one describes it as a mass media(ted) culture in which the same characters and concepts appear around the world not only in movies, books and television shows, but also in toys, games and other products. Chapter two catalogs some major characteristics of those media, characteristics now expected even in the liturgy and ministry of the church. Chapter three surveys the church's continuum of options for responding to electronic media. It argues that rejecting, challenging and adopting the mass media all have their moments (without losing the human moment of face-to-face communication).

The rest of the book discusses how and when ministers should do each, using media without being used by media. Chapter four suggests six spiritual reasons to fast from media during Lent and beyond, a sort of spiritual "cleansing of the palate" before you begin to engage media more intensely from a Christian perspective. Chapter five teaches how to "read" the mass media through two lenses, the lens of media literacy and the lens of the Christian Gospel. Chapter six tells how to share that knowledge within your parish or other ministry setting. Chapter seven is about preaching in a culture in which the stories of the mass media, especially television, have become more familiar than the stories of the Bible. Chapter eight focuses on using mass media, especially videos, in Christian formation of all kinds. Chapter nine gets into specifics of effectively taking your ministry online. Chapter ten, based on my own experience as a journalist and as a diocesan director of communications, offers advice for dealing with the press whether the news is good or bad. Chapter eleven suggests some spiritual exercises for this media age. Chapter twelve wraps it all up and sends you off to make new things happen in your ministry.

All of these chapters except the last two conclude with several reflection questions (for spirituality) and the book itself ends with a collection of resources (for practicality). The resource section is far from exhaustive. It is just a start, citing a few books, tapes and Web sites with which I'm familiar and think will be of help to pastoral ministers. Not even every book quoted is cited there, just the ones I think will have widespread interest. One more note on resources: In this fast-moving media world, there's unfortunately no guarantee that the Web sites listed are still in place as you read this. I thought it was important to include them, though, because Web sites have the capacity to be current, in-depth and interactive.

This book will not give you a prefabbed plan for using television, film and cyberspace in your ministry setting. Only you can decide how to use them, because only you know your ministry and your people. But this book will equip you with the tools you need to read the mass media in the light of the gospel and then use those media in your ministry. You will learn to challenge media but also remain open to what they have to tell the church. For that, let us pray:

> God of love and truth, your only son Jesus Christ is
> both the medium and the message by which you tell us
> that "God is with us"—Emmanuel. Through him, with
> him, in him may we become antennae communicating
> your world to the church, and your church to the
> world. Amen.

ONE

Our Mass Media(ted) Culture

The culture in which we live and minister, born in the U.S.A. and exported around the world, carries lots of labels. It's been called (in alphabetical order) an audiovisual culture, a commercial culture, a consumer culture, an electronic culture, an image culture and an information culture. All of those descriptions are fitting. But the one that fits best is a term that encompasses all of the others—a mass media culture or mass mediated culture.

Mass media both reflect and, increasingly, define what's becoming a world culture—the shared beliefs, values, traditions and conduct codes of our global community. In effect, they are our culture. And culture always helps shape religious knowledge, faith and practice.

Consider playwright Paul Rudnick's exposure to religion via popular culture. When he set out to rewrite the Bible as a satirical drama called *The Most Fabulous Story Ever Told*, he drew upon what he knew best—movies, television and a little bit of print. Rudnick wrote about this work in *The New York Times*:

I soon decided to base my play on my acquired notions
of the Bible, on a lifetime of "Davey and Goliath"
Saturday morning cartoons and the films of Cecil B.
DeMille, especially that moment in *The Ten Commandments*
where an MGM-gowned Anne Baxter remarks
something like, "You're a fool, Moses!" I also recalled
Richard Gere, hopping exultantly through the streets of
Jerusalem, clad only in a sort of Galilee diaper, in the
movie *King David*, musicals from *Jesus Christ Superstar*
to *Into the Night*, a notorious dud centering on the
Shroud of Turin, and a children's book called *Blintzes for
Blitzen*, in which a Jewish shopkeeper named Bernie
befriends a reindeer.

The mass media *mediated* the Bible for Rudnick, starting with
a Sunday morning religious television program for children.
No surprise there—TV is the most pervasive of the mass
media in terms of exposure. United States Census Bureau figures released in 1997 showed the average American spends
4.4 hours each day watching TV, 2.9 hours listening to the
radio, 45 minutes on recorded music, 27 minutes with a newspaper and 17 minutes on magazines. The Henry J. Kaiser
Family Foundation's 1999 survey, "Kids & Media @ The New
Millennium," found that the "typical American child" used
media five hours and 29 minutes per day, with half of that
time devoted to TV. That's almost as long as they spend each
day in a classroom—and TV doesn't take off for the summer
or holidays. Parents who think Catholic school for their children is important should reflect on the even larger day-to-day
role of mass media in those children's lives.

Anything or anyone that conveys something (such as a
message or an electronic impulse) is a medium. *You* are a
medium through which Christ reaches other people, for example. This book, however, is concerned primarily with electronic media and especially mass media, those media that
convey the same message to large numbers of people.
Television, films, radio and now the Internet are all mass
media. But I will be referring most often to television because
it's by far the most used of all media. In fact, TV watching is

the most popular leisure-time activity everywhere in the world. Ninety-eight percent of American homes have TV— essentially saturation level—and more than half of these have more than one television. Much of the rest of the world is similarly plugged in, even in underdeveloped countries. In China, for example, 89 percent of homes have televisions while only 2 percent have hot running water.

Ray Bradbury's vision of wall-TV's in his novel *Fahrenheit 451* has come true metaphorically. Television is the wallpaper (in the computer-age sense) of our lives. It's the running background sound not only in our homes, but in our schools, bars, restaurants, doctor's offices, hospital rooms, airports and now airplanes. It even invades our fantasy lives as a universally familiar prop in comic strips, greeting cards and—self-referentially—TV shows. A telephone poll of 600 teenagers conducted by the National Constitution Center in 1999 offers a window on what this means. Only 41 percent of U.S. teenagers polled could name the three branches of government, but 59 percent could name the Three Stooges. Nearly three-quarters could name the city where Bart Simpson lives (Springfield), but only 12 percent knew where Abraham Lincoln lived (also Springfield—Illinois.) I know a young man born in the early 1980's who uttered as his first full sentence the punch line of a TV commercial that was then highly popular: "Where's the beef?"

Even that minority of people who don't watch television, the TV teetotalers, is influenced by those in the great majority who do. Moreover, they get a strong dose of secondhand television through other media as well. So even living TV-free offers no inoculation against television's reach.

The Culture Industries Matrix

And yet television is just a part of a larger media environment, though a critical part because it is the most pervasive and most used. Television affects other media, and other media affect TV as they all cannibalize each other. Perhaps this is most easily seen in fictional plots and characters.

Virtually every popular character and storyline eventually appears on the TV screen, the movie screen and the computer screen. Its origin could be on any of those screens—or in another medium, such as a book or a comic strip. And the entire mediascape, including other electronic media and print, is part of a still-larger culture industries matrix.

THE CULTURE INDUSTRIES MATRIX

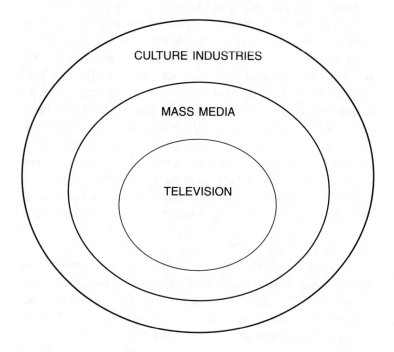

This matrix entwines the mass media with the commercial products that either spin off from or inspire media productions (toys, games, licensed characters) and the commercial marketplaces where they all come together (malls, theme parks). The Simpsons succeeded the Stooges on the lunch boxes of America; baby boomer TV shows from "The Dukes of Hazzard" to "Scooby Doo" have been resurrected as video games.

The relationships among these various components of the matrix, all products of the culture industries, are not linear. They move in all directions, influencing and being influenced by each other. Sometimes the distinctions among them disappear. The model for *USA Today*, with its heavy use of color and emphasis on entertainment, isn't other newspapers but television. It's even sold in boxes designed to look like TV sets. On the flip side, cable has made television a giant mall crammed with department stores (ABC, CBS, NBC, FOX, WB, UPN) and boutiques (The Science Fiction Network, The History Channel). And television programming is segmented for different interests like a newspaper. The axis around which the culture industries matrix revolves is advertising. Without it there would be no culture industries. Advertising not only sponsors programming in the electronic media, it's the reason those programs exist. Television's content—which could be defined as "the stuff sandwiched among the commercials"—is designed to deliver the largest possible audience, with the desired age and income profile, to the advertiser. That's what the advertiser is paying for.

But advertising is far more than commercials. Clothing with logos turns human beings into walking billboards. Licensed characters advertise the movie or television program on which they're based, and the movie advertises the toys, T-shirts, games and amusement park rides that bear its name. (Disney, Warner Brothers and now McDonald's have entire retail stores devoted to their licensed products.) Some half-hour cartoon shows are extended commercials for a toy upon which the program was based. MTV videos hype CD's and movies. Walt Disney's various hour-long television programs over the decades have been weekly ads for Disney theme parks, movies and toys. And it's difficult to buy a fast-food meal without also acquiring a movie tie-in toy.

MAJOR LINKS IN THE
CULTURE INDUSTRIES MATRIX

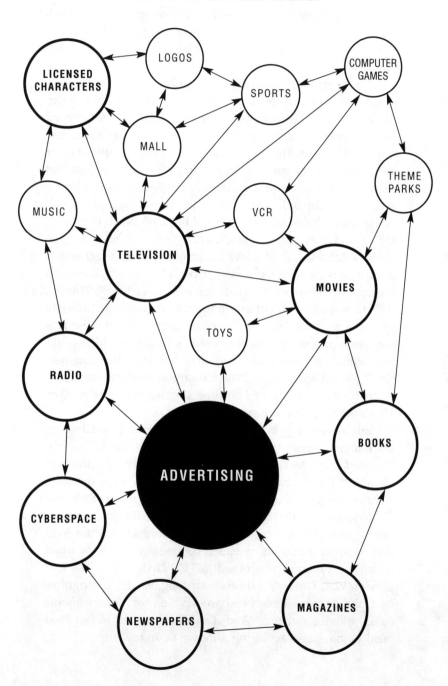

Seemingly one of the most anti-consumerist programs ever shown on television is the cartoon classic *A Charlie Brown Christmas*, which says the real meaning of Christmas appears in Luke 2 rather than in purchased goods. Yet it features a set of popular comic strip characters that appear in millions of dollars worth of books, videos, games, toys and greeting cards for sale at Christmas. The program is a kind of commercial for all of that, and the products in turn are commercials for the annual Christmas special. The production of new "Peanuts" strips ended when cartoonist Charles Schulz retired and then died early in 2000, but Charlie Brown's commercial empire continues.

Multimedia, Unified Message

The message of consumerist values is the same, regardless of the medium. Critics frequently blame the fact that a handful of transnational corporations dominate the global media market, many with interests in nearly every segment of the culture industries matrix. General Electric, Disney, Westinghouse, Time Warner (even before the proposed merger with America Online), Sony, News Corp., Viacom, Seagram and Bertelsmann don't leave much of the mediasphere for any other companies to own. The only corporations as influential in the media are major advertisers such as Coca-Cola, McDonald's and Nike, whose names and logos are as familiar worldwide as Mickey Mouse.

That concentration is troubling, but probably makes little difference in the product content. If the top nine media companies were ninety companies, they would still produce the same stuff because the ultimate goal is the same for all—to make money. And to make money from movies, books, television, radio, magazines, newspapers, CD's, video games or the Internet, it's essential to attract an audience. The pursuit of audience market share sparks less innovation than imitation as all the players attempt to be entertaining, stimulating (that is, often sexual and violent) and yet comforting. In such an economy there's no room for challenging a value system that says you are what you own. Consumption is the engine driving the entire matrix; advertising is just the ignition key.

Many Christian critics rightly challenge the global culture industries' values of consumerism, instant gratification and will-to-power as being in direct conflict with the Beatitudes of Jesus (Matthew 5:3-12). In fact, if religion is "a belief in what saves us and gives us ultimate meaning," as John Kavanaugh, S.J., has defined it, then the programming, the advertising, the toys and the icons of the culture industries offer a kind of competing religion to the Judeo-Christian ethic. Don't be too sure you know which religion you've chosen yourself. The University of Dayton's Sister Fran Trampiets suggests that a good examination of conscience question for our age would be: Am I being formed by the mass media or am I being formed by the word of God?

Are the two *always* in opposition? Not at all! Since Pope Pius XI's encyclical letter *Vigilanti Cura* in 1936, which said that films can exercise "a profoundly moral influence upon those who see them" (25), the church has recognized the positive role of electronic media as well as the dangers. Even though secular programs are produced with the primary purpose of making money, they can also entertain, educate and edify. UNDA-USA, the national Catholic association for communicators, each year presents its Gabriel Awards to film, television and radio productions that uplift the human spirit.

Just as Jesus talked about separating the wheat from the weeds after they had grown together for a while, we need to practice discernment as consumers of mass media. That means sifting out good from bad instead of unreflectively accepting whatever shows up on the screen or unreflectively condemning. The process is to first identify the values embodied in the program—even a sitcom has them—and compare them to the values and virtues that Jesus embodies in the gospel. It will help if you come to that task with an understanding of the different ways in which media affect both culture and religious faith.

Pushing the Culture, Changing the Faith

The mass media reflect the culture—that's why they're "mass"—but they also push it. They eventually turn the marginal into the mainstream by persistently emphasizing the new, the unexpected and especially the shocking in their drive to build market share. What's over-the-top in a film this year is commonplace in films next year and acceptable, or at least tolerated, in neighborhoods a decade or so later.

Religious beliefs and practices aren't isolated from the tug of the culture industries. After all, most folks spend a lot more time in front of the tube than they do in front of the altar—seven times as much if they go to church once every week and watch TV only an hour a day. Is it any wonder that TV may form their theology more than church does? I know a highly educated and active Catholic who, probably nurtured by years of watching *It's a Wonderful Life* on TV, is convinced that good people become angels when they die.

But it's not only the content of mass media that influences a culture or a religious tradition. The form, or technology, may have an even greater impact. To say (as I did earlier) that the message is the same regardless of the medium because the culture industries share ownership and values is not to dispute the importance of the medium. In a phrase coined and popularized by media guru Marshall McLuhan in the early 1960's, "The medium is the message." Each medium has its own language. And as anyone who's studied another language knows, languages are never completely translatable. The message changes a bit with the language. This is as true of Christianity as of any other message. The Christian gospel has been reshaped by the media that have transmitted it— oral, manuscript, print and electronic.

Those media, as McLuhan frequently noted, each heralded and advanced the creation of a new culture. "No one of these cultures has perfectly served the goals of Christianity," says theologian Avery Dulles, S.J., "but all of them could be, and were, used to some effect." In a talk to an audience of Catholic communicators, Dulles outlined how various communication cultures have affected Christianity:

The oral culture supported the authority of the prophet or preacher, including the early Christian witnesses. Peter, Paul and other apostles summarized the *kerygma* in brief confessional statements such as "Jesus is risen, Jesus is Lord," backed up by the personal authority of their apostolic witness. Communities of disciples accepted the Gospel. "Oral culture therefore served well for purposes of Christian proclamation," Dulles says. "But for assuring the permanence and universality of the faith and for inculcating the fine points of doctrine, the spoken word was insufficient. Already in the earliest period it was supplemented by other means, especially the canonical Scriptures."

In the manuscript culture of the Middle Ages, the focus of authority shifted definitively from oral proclamation to the written texts of the Bible and the writings of the Fathers of the Church. "The bottom line was no longer, 'I say unto you,' but rather, 'It is written.' " But because manuscripts were rare and most Christians illiterate, sacred art, drama and music supplemented the written word.

The print culture put the Bible into the hands of millions, weakened the authority of the Roman church, and fueled the Reformation. Both Catholics and Protestants churned out previously unimaginable quantities of Bibles, catechisms and polemical tracts. The locus of authority gradually shifted again, "from the sacred text to the authors, who claimed authority to produce texts of their own," Dulles says. "In the so-called 'age of reason,' theology itself was obliged to become rational and critical, borrowing the weapons of its adversaries. The church was on the defensive."

Dulles correctly characterizes our current communications culture as "multimedia, with the recognition that electronic transmission is dominant." He notes that print remains, "oral proclamation is experiencing a certain revival" through electronic reproduction, and music holds an important place in the electronic culture.

New Media, New Meanings

If past is prologue, Dulles's historical survey leaves little room for doubt that what he calls the multimedia culture—the culture industries' output and the media in which those cultural productions are embodied—will have an impact on the church as profound as that of earlier communication cultures. Neil Postman recognizes this when he says in his neo-Luddite book *Technopoly*: "A preacher who confines himself to considering how a medium can increase his audience will miss the significant question: In what sense do new media alter what is meant by religion, by church, even by God?" That's a question for every minister. And it's the question that got this book started.

Communications theorists may argue with Postman's apparent assumption that baby boomers and Generation Xers, Anglos and Hispanics, men and women (to name just a few demographic groups) all mean the same things by the terms religion, church and God, and that they're all affected the same way by the new media. That misses the point. All ages and races and both sexes swim in the same culture. They may be affected differently and in different degrees by the dominance of electronic media, in part because their exposure differs. (The latchkey children of Generation X saw a lot more television than their parents and grandparents did, for example.) But they're all affected in some way—just as their ancestors were all affected by the inventions of alphabetic writing and the printed book.

The culture industries, largely through the electronic media, truly have changed the definitions and expectations of religion, church and God. To find out how and to what degree, we'll first identify the key characteristics common to electronic media and look at how they've affected religious faith and practice. With that knowledge, we can begin to discern how ministers of the church can be relevant to a mass mediated culture and yet faithful to the Gospel of Jesus Christ.

For Reflection

- *How am I being formed by the word of God—or how am I being formed by the mass media?*

- *What are the Beatitudes of the mass media culture? Who does this culture say is happy or blessed?*

- *How do those Beatitudes compare to the Beatitudes of Jesus (Matthew 5:3-12)?*

TWO

Screen Saved?

Religious educators around the globe and across denominational lines are realizing the importance of media literacy and are incorporating its principles into their programs. They recognize the necessity of being able to read "the signs of the times" (Matthew 16:1-3) in the mass media and respond, if one is to be a Christian in a mass-mediated culture. But in examining the media as a sort of Rosetta stone for the culture, these good scholars and ministers seldom question the *impact* of the culture industries—the mass media and the manufacturers of interrelated consumer goods—on religious faith and practice. Christian religious educators and media literacy theorists haven't considered deeply enough how people look at church, and what they look for from church, in this media age.

In considering Neil Postman's question—"In what sense do new media alter what is meant by religion, by church, even by God?"—we may think first of the storylines in the mass media (both news and entertainment) that embody particular moral values, attitudes toward religion and depictions of clergy. Those values, attitudes and depictions tend in the same direction throughout the media—away from tradition and toward "what is new, different and surprising," as Avery Dulles put it. This is particularly true of the electronic media which "screen" reality for most Westerners—through the television screen, the movie screen, the computer screen. Over time, their persistently delivered messages seem to be turning the *avant garde* into the everyday, even among religious believers, thus accelerating trends already present in the culture.

But the relatively rare storylines explicitly dealing with religion aren't the only way that electronic media affect religious belief and practice. They also alter our approach to doctrine, worship and theology by their very nature, even when they're not dealing with such subjects. The media's key characteristics, many of them related to the form of the electronic media or to unity of form and content rather than to content alone, pervade Western popular culture because the media do. Westerners have become so used to these characteristics that they expect to find them everywhere—in school, at the mall, in politics, even in religion, church and God. This is a change at least as big as the switch to personal interpretation of the Bible brought about by Gutenberg's introduction of print culture. Eventually, as we shall see, changed expectations lead to changed definitions.

Electronic media generally are visual, aural, commercial, entertaining, stimulating, novel, affective, comforting, simplistic, validating, democratic, controllable and interactive, disembodied, atomizing and immediate. Not every medium has all of these characteristics all the time, but they apply in general and to electronic media as a whole. And commercial television has all of them most of the time. Largely because of television, these characteristics have become intrinsic to Western culture as well. Let's take a closer look at each.

Electronic Media Are Visual. Images in Western culture are as common as television screens, and getting more so with the proliferation of personal computers. Photos or drawings on a computer screen can be downloaded or forwarded in an

E-mail with a few clicks of a mouse. Lectures just as easily become multimedia presentations with PowerPoint. A television commercial for a chain of photocopying stores portrayed a young man using full-color flow charts and diagrams to convince his dinner partner that he's a credible prospect for marriage.

Television, movie and computer screens aren't the only media that deliver images. So do books, magazines, photographs, comics, corporate logos, greeting cards, cereal boxes and action figures. Even medieval manuscripts were gloriously illustrated. But the invention of dry-plate photography in the nineteenth century launched what historian Daniel Boorstin calls "the Graphic Revolution." The New England essayist Oliver Wendell Holmes believed that in the age of photography "image would become more important than the object itself, and would in fact make the object disposable." If he meant that the Mona Lisa would lose its value because anyone can own a cheap copy, he clearly was wrong. But if he meant that the image would become more important than the reality, he may well have been right. Tourists to the Grand Canyon reportedly are skipping the canyon itself in droves to watch a big-screen theater presentation of the canyon at the site instead. Why? Because the big screen, the camera angles, the fast cuts are more exciting.

So visual images can trump reality. They also communicate in ways that words don't, and may at times contradict and override words. Even when the words are true and the image isn't, the image may be what sticks. Seeing *is* believing. Journalist James Fallows, in his book *Breaking the News: How the Media Undermine American Democracy,* describes a Reagan Administration spinmeister congratulating CBS television reporter Lesley Stahl. She had put together a segment which, though highly critical of administration policy, showed the President in positive poses—speaking at a Special Olympics competition and appearing at ceremonies opening a nursing home. "Don't you people realize that the picture is all that counts?" the official asked Stahl.

Electronic Media Are Aural. Electronic communication has always had an audio dimension, from the clicking out of Morse code on the first telegraphs to "You've Got Mail!" and RealAudio on home computers. Since the visual has been a part of every post-oral method of communication, this stimulation of the ear is what makes the audiovisual era different from those that preceded it. Communications theorists call ours a "secondary oral" culture for reasons easy to see—and hear. Millions of people "read" books on tape while driving or jogging. "I hear you" has become a common way of saying, "I understand." The "on" button is the default mode for televisions in most American homes not because of the pictures coming from it but because of the sounds that give the illusion of company and drive out the loneliness. Silence itself sometimes seems to be the enemy in Western culture.

Electronic Media Are Commercial. When Philo T. Farnsworth publicly demonstrated his invention of television for the first time in 1927, he broadcast a dollar bill for sixty seconds. His choice of image was emblematic of the way television and other electronic media have developed, particularly in the United States. They are all about selling stuff. Even supposedly non-commercial "public" radio and television have products to push, as anyone on the mailing list for the *Wireless* and *Signals* catalogues knows. At least one public television station has its own store selling PBS-related videos, dolls, games and clothing, just like a Disney or Warner Brothers store.

The epitome of commercial media is MTV, which began as an entire network built on commercials called music videos. But MTV isn't the only place on the airwaves where the lines are blurred. Television is adopting the practice, long established in films, of "product placement"—accepting money for using brand name products on fictional programs. The result? In her book *The Overspent American*, Harvard economist Juliet Schor cites research showing that the more television a person watches the more he or she spends. Whether viewers buy the particular products being advertised or not, television is a cheerleader for consumption. Ditto the World Wide Web.

And it doesn't stop there. In addition to selling consumer goods and the consumer culture, electronic media also sell the values that they've grafted onto those products through advertising (sex appeal, strength, beauty, wealth, prestige and hipness).

Electronic Media Are Entertaining. Postman, in his seminal book *Amusing Ourselves to Death*, says television is at the center of "a culture in which all public discourse increasingly takes the form of entertainment," including religion. The VCR and the remote control have made television even more of an amusement-on-demand medium, but not the only one.

One of America's most entertaining and successful writers of popular fiction, Michael Crichton, has a character in his 1999 novel *Timeline* say that entertainment has become the dominant mode of experience in every field "from politics to marketing to education."

> Today, everybody expects to be entertained, and they
> expect to be entertained all the time. Business meetings
> must be snappy, with bullet lists and animated graphics,
> so executives aren't bored. Malls and stores must be
> engaging, so they amuse us as well as sell us. Politicians
> must have pleasing video personalities and tell us only
> what we want to hear. Schools must be careful not to
> bore young minds that expect the speed and complexity
> of television. Students must be amused—everyone must
> be amused, or they will switch: switch brands, switch
> channels, switch parties, switch loyalties.

Entertainment value enters into journalistic decisions about what to cover as news and how to cover it. It shouldn't have been so surprising that *ABC News* sent superstar actor Leonardo DiCaprio instead of a reporter to interview President Clinton about global warming for an Earth Day 2000 broadcast.

All electronic media have an entertainment bias, with which they've infected the culture. We'll see that manifested in many of the remaining characteristics of electronic media that we consider.

Electronic Media Are Stimulating. The word "stimulating" can mean a lot of different things. And in the case of electronic media, it does.

First of all, the ubiquitous and constant presence of electronic media permits no "down time" from media. Most notably, television is simply everywhere. We stare all day long at TV sets in restaurants, bars, airports, airplanes, medical offices, classrooms, church halls and even sanctuaries. In Japan, a media-saturated nation like the United States, the taxicabs have little televisions mounted below the dashboard. Where there isn't a television, there is often a radio, CD player, computer or cell phone. How many of these media have you used today? How many have you seen or heard in the hands of others? Cardinal James A. Hickey of Washington, D.C., felt compelled to write a column in his archdiocesan newspaper, *The Catholic Standard*, to say: "Turn your cell phones off in church. Use the occasion to recharge the batteries in your cell phone and the spiritual batteries in yourselves."

Another way media stimulate is by titillating the senses. Television programs and commercials, influenced by MTV, thrive on loud sounds, fast scene changes, special effects, shocking words and scenes. Dolls talk and move, and magazine ads are laced with appealing fragrances. The evening news on television is not just the news, but "Action News" and "Live!" Movies and Broadway plays have to be spectacles, and special effects attract more comment than plot.

The biggest way that television, music videos, video games and even comic books stimulate is through ever heavier doses and ever more graphic portrayals of sex and violence. The doses must increase and the images become more graphic because, as with an addictive drug, it takes more to achieve the same level of stimulation, spectacle, vibration. A clue to the importance of sex and violence in holding television viewers is the emphasis on those elements in commercials for upcoming episodes. Some of the sexiest and most violent minutes on the tube are the commercials for TV shows.

Electronic Media Are Novel. Perhaps the most frequently used word in electronic media is "new," whether warranted or not. In this the media reflect but also reaffirm the neomania of the culture, modernity's assumption that what is new is automatically better.

Electronic Media Are Affective. Electronic media appeal to emotions rather than to the intellect. They're non-rational. The printed page is by nature linear, giving order to the world. But the fast-moving and disjointed electronic media portray a nonlinear world that—if entertaining—is also incoherent, unmanageable and illogical.

Cutting across form and content, this is equally true of action films, situation comedies, video games and World Wide Web sites. But the apex is advertising. Ads seldom offer an argument for buying a product. Indeed, it's not always clear what product the ad is selling. The focus is usually on happy, active, attractive people, visually implying that buying the advertiser's jeans or cigarettes will make one what they are.

Electronic Media Are Comforting. One of the unspoken guidelines of content in advertiser-sponsored media is "Do Not Disturb." Disturbing the viewer is bad for business because it could provoke a channel switch. Sentimental sadness in a TV drama is okay, but challenging the social order does not sell luxury cars. Films have a little more leeway to be discomforting.

Electronic Media Are Simplistic. In the film *Pleasantville*, the black and white world of a 1950's television show starts turning into living color with the arrival of two 1990's teenagers from the other side of the screen. In reality, TV is still black and white, and so are other electronic media. Like comic strips and comic books, they make sense of the world by simplistically reducing it to binary opposites of good/evil, sacred/profane, right/wrong and us/them. They resolve issues clearly and finally. Consider what happens when a book becomes a Disney movie: Characters become caricatures. Hercules is an action figure with product endorsements, and the Hunchback

of Notre Dame (without the dark side we remember from earlier incarnations) lives happily ever after at the end of the
movie.

This didn't start with electronic media. In 1922, journalist Walter Lippmann wrote in his book *Public Opinion* about
the mass media resort to stereotypes, a term he drew from
the printing trade of his day. But electronic media rely on
stereotypes even more than did the newspapers in
Lippmann's era. Script writers and video game creators save
time and effort on character development by using familiar
types instead of three-dimensional characters. Women,
minorities and ethnic groups in particular are easily and frequently stereotyped in films, sitcoms and commercials. But
white men are typecast, too, in the templates of macho action
heroes, dominating husbands or bosses, or the bumbling
idiots of sitcoms.

Electronic Media Are Validating. The electronic media have
become the ultimate means for validating the true, the real,
the important. Cecilia Tichi applies the term "certification" to
the validation that products and people gain by being on television. " 'As seen on TV' has been a mark and stamp from
the early 1950's, appearing in the United States on products
from toys to kitchenware to clothing," she notes in *Electronic
Hearth: Creating an American Television Culture*. In the movie
Forrest Gump, every time the eponymous hero reaches some
pinnacle of achievement it is broadcast on television—the
filmmaker's way of validating the event's (and Forrest's)
importance.

This validating role of mass media isn't limited to fictional
television and to movies. Readers and watchers of "the news"
tacitly assume that the news is what happened of importance
that day—so if it wasn't reported, it wasn't important. And
advertising says that buying this product or, just as likely, this
brand name will validate or certify me as a human being.
"You Are What You Drink," a Diet Coke commercial assures
us. A brand name doesn't just brand a product. It also
"brands" the consumer, transferring the values imputed to

that product to the one who consumes it. Consumers are encouraged to—and do—define themselves in part by the labels they wear, drink or drive.

Electronic Media Are Democratic. The grade-level distinctions imposed by books simply don't apply to television. Children and adults watch many of the same programs. In this and other ways, electronic media are accessible to all. You don't need to be literate to watch television or films, a corporation to publish on the Internet, a broadcasting personality to have a voice on talk radio, or a titan of television to produce a cable access program. That's not to say that a fifth-grader with a camcorder and big-money CBS are equally likely to attract an audience on television or in cyberspace. But they do have an equal chance to "make media." So does the church.

Another way electronic media are democratic is that all spectacle is somewhat equal on TV or the Internet. The concept of importance gets forgotten. When O.J. Simpson lost a civil verdict in the death of his wife, the decision shared a split screen on at least one TV network with the president of the United States arriving to deliver his State of the Union address. The screen image put the final chapter of a real-life soap opera on a par with a constitutionally mandated duty of the world's most powerful leader.

Distinctions based on authority tend to get leveled out in cyberspace. As different voices come through the same electronic channels directly into the home, they may be accorded the same weight. Or if one has an edge, it's based on graphics rather than the authority of the source. The Heaven's Gate religious cult that led 39 people to mass suicide in March, 1997, had its own colorful Web page, and it was glitzier than the Vatican's. A French Catholic bishop at odds with Rome over issues of both doctrine and discipline set up a "virtual diocese" in cyberspace by launching a Web site under the name of his titular see after being removed from leadership of his real-world diocese. Both authorship and authority get lost in cyberspace. This is different from a book culture in which the authority of the author or an *imprimatur* (whether from ecclesiastical or cultural authorities) confers credibility.

Yet another sense in which mass media are democratic is that they respond to the desires of their audiences. That's a commercial necessity if they're to sustain those audiences and thus attract advertising dollars (which go where the customers are). For all the complaints about the quality of television, millions of people are still watching. And if not enough people are watching a particular show, it's gone.

Electronic Media Are Controllable and Interactive. Television, radio and the Internet are electronic malls, offering an array of consumer choices to be checked out with the click of a mouse, a pre-set button or a remote control device. Consumer choice and instant gratification reign. A young friend once told my daughter, "With cable, there's always something better on." The viewer or listener is a consumer, and the consumer is in control with a magic wand called "the remote." The VCR adds another layer of control by making it possible to tape programs broadcast at times inconvenient for the viewer and watch them when it is convenient.

Quentin J. Schultze notes in his book *Internet for Christians* that Internet surfers create their own experience—two may enter a Web site at the same time, but then follow different links to other Web sites. Television viewers also surf, in effect creating their own story lines in search of entertainment. That makes even television interactive, although it's often thought of as a passive medium.

Interactivity is even easier to notice in Internet chat rooms, talk radio call-in shows and video games. Their interactivity puts the consumer in charge, makes them controllable.

Electronic Media Are Disembodied. You can't really "reach out and touch someone" with a telephone call, and E-mail is even more removed from the person generating it because you can't hear the voice or even see the handwriting of the sender. (My wife feels a strong emotional connection to recipes written in the handwriting of her mother and other deceased loved ones.) Joshua Meyrowitz argues throughout his book

No Sense of Place that electronic media such as television, radio, telephones and "personal sound systems" have reduced the significance of physical presence.

This separation of the message and the messenger has been with us a long time. It began with the foundation of all electronic media, the telegraph. The first newspaper to use the telegraph to transmit news—just one day after Samuel F.B. Morse demonstrated the invention—commented, "This is indeed the annihilation of space."

The disembodiment of electronic media reaches its apex (so far) in cyberspace and virtual reality, where you can be not only anywhere and nowhere but anyone and no one. The stories of cyberspace deceptions, with consequences ranging from comic to tragic, are the stuff of urban legend—except that many are true. As a famous *New Yorker* cartoon illustrates, "On the Internet, nobody knows you're a dog." Nor does anyone know you're poor, female, of color, elderly, handicapped or don't speak English well. Shedding those differences based on socioeconomic levels, gender and other characteristics that cannot be perceived through the computer screen is part of cyberspace's attraction for some. It's another manifestation of the democratic nature of electronic media.

Diverse writers have used similar language to report the sensation of forgetting that they have a body while in cyberspace. Of course, the body is still involved: you have to use hands to type messages in cyberspace—or maybe your mouth and voice box to pronounce words into a voice recognition system. It's only the awareness of the body that fades. Some enthusiasts not only acknowledge this separation of person and body, they revel in it and write about using computers to escape the body.

Electronic Media Are Atomizing. Just as electronic media separate the human person from physical realities such as place and body, they also separate people from each other. When you see a person walking down the street with his or her ear attached to a radio, a cell phone, a Walkman or maybe even a personal television, you know that person is in relationship with that medium, not with others on the street. Several media critics have called this effect "atomizing," the opposite of unifying.

At home, television began its life as the electronic hearth around which the family gathered. It brought family members together. Today, with most families owning multiple sets, it often pulls them apart. How many television sets do you have in your home? It's not uncommon for my college students to report as many as seven. My wife, asking that question of her seventh-grade students, has received answers as high as ten. In a poll by the organization Children Now, 54 percent of the children responding said they have a television in their own room, and 55 percent said they watch alone or with friends but not with family. The Henry J. Kaiser Family Foundation's "Kids & Media @ The New Millennium" report, which surveyed 3,000 youngsters between the ages of 2 and 18, found that 65 percent of those age 8 and older had TVs in their bedrooms and 21 percent had bedroom computers. Important lessons about negotiation and accommodation—necessities when families have to share one television set or one computer—are lost in these families.

It's not only the multiplication of TV sets that atomizes, but also the proliferation of programming sources and the nature of the programming. With cable and satellite TV offering dozens of channels, and the video store down the street thousands of movies, particular programs are less likely to be shared cultural experiences than they were during the era of network domination. Entire cable networks are directed at such narrow niches (but strong target markets) as science fiction fans or home and garden enthusiasts. Even the mainstream shows on old-line networks are skewed to particular demographic groups that advertisers want to reach. For example, a brochure from CBS Marketing informs potential advertisers that " 'Touched by an Angel' delivers higher concentrations of 25-54 consumers of a wide range of products than NBC's 'Friends.' "

While many devotees perceive cyberspace as bringing them into "virtual community," a unifying rather than atomizing function, virtual community is very different from real community. If it weren't, there wouldn't need to be a special name for it. The Web is a wonderful source of entertainment, information, and even pre-evangelization; the church needs to be there. E-mail is fantastic for linking family and friends separated by miles or continents, not to mention organizing E-mail prayer chains as some have done. In the hierarchy of human communications, however, E-mail can only augment but not replace embodied human contact. Body language, tone of voice, the sound of laughter, a warm smile, a friendly touch all are all missing online. I have friends that I message via E-mail every few days, but I still want to visit them in person and be co-present with them sometimes.

For some people, though, E-mail may be squeezing out person-to-person contact. A Stanford University study in 2000 found that a quarter of the survey respondents who spent five hours or more a week on the Internet reported reducing their in-person and telephone interactions with friends or family. That finding seemed to dovetail with an earlier Carnegie Mellon University study of online users which indicated that people who spent even a few hours a week in cyberspace suffered higher levels of loneliness and depression than others. But another study in 2000 by the Pew Internet and American Life Project found Internet users actually more likely to interact with other people face to face. So does the Internet bring people together or pull them apart? Probably both.

Critics of the Carnegie and Stanford research emphasize the Internet's capacity to forge new friendships or maintain existing ones through its interactive elements. But some of the functions of cyberspace may actually pull society apart in a larger sense even while bringing people together. For example, the chat rooms, bulletin boards and list serves built around particular interests seem to confirm like-minded individuals in their opinions more often than exposing them to new ones. This doesn't have to happen, but it can happen. (The same could be said of social clubs and talk radio.) And when Internet habitués create virtual newspapers tailored to their own narrow interests, as various services enable them to do, they are simultaneously opting out of learning about the broader world. The Web plays to individualism, or at best small-group pursuits, whereas a habit of more general reading informs concern for the common good. Electronic media (cell phones, beepers, E-mail) bring people into connection, but they don't and can't bring community.

Electronic Media Are Immediate. Electronic media provide quick access to information, entertainment—and people. In a well-worn phrase, the remote-control clicker, the pre-set button on the car radio, the beeper, and call waiting are all tools of instant gratification. So are E-mail's "instant message" function and the availability of news round-the-clock on the Internet.

The bias of the technology toward speed and access carries over into the content: Television commercials and sitcoms deliver fast and often painless solutions to problems, while reporters broadcast breathlessly from the scene—*live!*—moments after an event (whether they have any facts to report yet or not). In an electronic culture, immediacy becomes more important than reflection or depth of communication, and makes them impossible. The result often is what Greg Howard's comic strip "Sally Forth" aptly called "artificial urgency" (January 1997).

As a culture, we don't like to wait for anything, whether it's dinner or intimacy. We're a society of fast food and instant millionaires. Electronic media both play to that desire and feed it.

Implications for the Church

These fifteen characteristics of electronic media are by no means all bad. Many are neutral or positive in the proper context and in the proper balance. Entertainment is a perfectly valid reason for a movie, for example. It's okay for a TV sitcom to be comforting and simplistic. And interactivity makes the Internet a powerful tool for gathering information and keeping in contact. But all of these characteristics, whether good, bad or neutral in themselves, can be problematic when they are expected to apply to the church.

Commentators frequently contend that mass media—films, television and now the Internet—have replaced the church as interpreter and meaning-maker. This is certainly true for millions of people deeply immersed in popular culture while hardly connected at all to the church. But while the mass media have assumed some of the roles of the church, the reverse is also true. Residents of Western cultures, for whom mass media are pervasive and inescapable in everyday life, now often attach mass-media expectations to the church experience. Orthodoxy and orthopraxy are less important, and the Spirit is more a special effect than a Presence. And some church leaders are buying in.

Protestant services, with their emphasis on the word, are inherently *aural*. Roman Catholic and Orthodox services, with their color-coded vestments and ritual actions, are inherently *visual*. Yet this doesn't seem enough for some congregations. Protestant ministers have illustrated sermons with TV or film clips, and Catholic parishes have shown slides at the communion meditation. Such actions do not merely draw images and techniques from the world of entertainment, they emulate it. They conform to what Postman calls "The Age of Show Business."

A flyer for one new non-denominational church promises comfort, consumer choice and, yes, entertainment. It touts "upbeat and contemporary music," "practical messages which encourage and challenge you each week," special services for the children, and an Easter egg hunt with "Over 10,000 Easter eggs, nationally known children's entertainers." Leaders of this church are responding to the demands of their market, the demand that church be *entertaining* and *comforting*. More established parishes in mainstream denominations recognize that and respond, too, especially during the pew-packing Christmas and Easter services. "The annual Christmas cantata does not appear to be enough anymore," religion columnist Stephen Huba wrote in *The Cincinnati Post*. "Now we need a multimedia event."

Tex Sample, a seminary professor and church growth enthusiast, would make every Sunday a multimedia event. His *affective* and *stimulating* ideal service, which he describes in his aptly titled book *The Spectacle of Worship in a Wired World*, begins this way: "In the gathering the band begins with a fast-paced version of 'Will the Circle Be Unbroken?' The words are displayed on the screen to allow the congregation to sing with the leadership team. Lights flash across the congregation in a layered way. That is, different colors of light sweep across different rows of seats."

Sample may be pushing the envelope, but he's pushing it in the same direction it's already moving in many parishes. And the unrecognized model is television—not televangelism, but television in general. If the congregation or the liturgy planners view the service as a show, and sometimes as a multimedia production, then the presider inevitably assumes the role of the genial star, whether the service is live or broadcast. The audience, like the TV audience, is looking for a comforting presence. That quest for comfort has caused many non-denominational megachurches to discard the cross as a central symbol in the sanctuary.

In the quest for greater congregational market share, some churches and even denominations downplay dogma. Have they become nothing more than brand names with only marketing—the appeal to target audiences and their felt needs— to distinguish them? The church that offers Easter eggs and children's entertainers also promises in its flyer "to meet your needs as we go into the new century." At Willow Creek Community Church near Chicago, the biggest congregation in America, a sign outside the chief pastor's office reads, "What is our business? Who is our customer? What does our customer value?"

Asking these marketing questions strongly implies that the answers will lead to customer-driven programming, just as on ABC, NBC, CBS and Fox. Whether that's good ecclesiology or not doesn't seem to matter—it's certainly good business. Churches are expected to be *democratic* and *controllable*, like television and cyberspace, even in terms of their teaching. If they're not, the worshiper always maintains control of where to worship. It's the consumer who's in control; not God. Christians—even Catholics, who were once immutably bound to a parish by geography—surf parishes as they do TV channels or the Internet. And if they don't find the programming sufficiently entertaining and comforting, they can change parishes almost as easily. While it might be claiming too much to insist that electronic media created this mindset, it's not a stretch to argue that they reinforce it.

Less obviously, perhaps, "cafeteria Catholics" and other "salad bar Christians" apply the prerogative of consumer choice to church doctrine as well. Wade Clark Roof, in his well known *A Generation of Seekers: The Spiritual Journeys of the Baby Boom Generation,* reported that "boomers look for congregations with certain attractions—one being a widespread preference for churches and synagogues that are tolerant, more open than closed on lifestyle issues." Even among conservative Protestants, almost half responding to Roof's survey opposed teaching of an absolute morality. The experience of surfing Web sites which put Christian teachings on a level playing field with Scientology, paganism and New Age spiritualities can only confirm this religious relativism.

The relationship between church and the Web or television is more than analogous for that relatively small group of persons who attempt to find their community of worship in a disembodied way, through religious broadcasting or an online church. Electronic services meet the new need to be constantly connected electronically, which we have observed with E-mail, cell phones and so on. But they don't truly bring community. Community implies responsibility to other embodied persons, not just accountability to rules of cyberspace "netiquette." That responsibility is missing on the Internet and may be avoided in megachurches. An indication that participation in online Christianity doesn't satisfy the human need for community is Scottish researcher Heidi Campbell's 1998 finding that it isn't causing participants to abandon their local places of worship. But to the extent that it pulls them out of the local church on a day to day basis, the cyberchurch still has an *atomizing* effect.

All churches are affected by the expectations of the mass-mediated culture in which they minister, from those that exist only in cyberspace to those that don't even have a Web page. The difference is that some know it and some don't.

For Reflection

- *What have you seen in the mass media in the past week that was presented as unexceptional but your faith tells you is unacceptable?*

- *When do you feel that liturgies should be more entertaining?*

- *How do electronic media connect you to or separate you from other people?*

THREE

The Church Responds

Clearly, some churches have consciously changed the way they do ministry and liturgy to meet the changed expectations of a mass-mediated culture. But that's not the only possible course. How *should* the church, and churches, respond to the world created by the culture industries? The question is essentially the same one that always faces the church as she struggles to work out her relationship with the culture. Varied answers have been put forward by Christian thinkers throughout the ages.

The best known attempt to categorize the church's options in relating to the culture is H. Richard Niebuhr's classic *Christ and Culture*. In this book Niebuhr, an influential Protestant theologian during the middle of the twentieth century, identifies five possible responses to the culture, citing advantages and disadvantages for each:

1) *Christ against culture*. Christians should separate themselves from the culture and its evil. This is the approach of 1 John and of the early Christian writer Tertullian, Christian monastics, and the novelist Leon Tolstoy. Niebuhr calls them radicals or exclusivists. We might also think of

them as separatists.

2) *Christ of culture.* "Christ is identified with what men conceive to be their finest ideals, their noblest institutions, and their best philosophy," Niebuhr explains. Distinctively Christian principles vanish. This is the approach of the gnostics (a heretical movement in the early church that considered the body and all physical matter to be essentially evil), Abelard, Thomas Jefferson and Immanuel Kant. Niebuhr calls them cultural Christians.

3) *Christ above culture.* This answers the problem of Christ and culture with a "both-and" ("Render unto Caesar . . ."), but places Christ far above culture. This is the approach of Saint Justin Martyr, Clement of Alexandria and Saint Thomas Aquinas. Niebuhr calls them synthesists.

4) *Christ and culture in paradox.* This is also a "both-and" view, but a more pessimistic one that emphasizes the conflict between grace in God and sin in human beings. Law in a Christian society prevents sin from being as destructive as it might be otherwise, but it isn't the positive good the synthesists see. Christians live a life of faith in tension between the demands of Christ and the demands of the culture. This is the approach of Saint Paul and Martin Luther. Niebuhr calls them dualists.

5) *Christ transforming culture.* With Christ, the Word entered culture. Christ is the converter and transformer of human action. This is the approach of Saint John the Evangelist, Saint Augustine, John Calvin and John Wesley. Niebuhr calls them conversionists.

The first two viewpoints that Neibuhr outlines are at exact opposite ends of the spectrum, while the final three represent shades of difference in the center.

Religion columnist Terry Mattingly updates Neibuhr with his own list of five ways the church responds to culture:

1) *Burn the culture.* This is the "separatist" option.

2) *"Baptize" the culture.* Adopt modern trends as the test of truth—theology by opinion poll. The left may "baptize" the culture on sexual issues; the right may "baptize" the culture on economic and military issues.

3) *Photocopy the culture*. Copy cultural trends, but make them Christian—as in Christian radio, TV and video; Christian heavy metal and rap; Christian self-help books.

4) *Change the culture*. Engage in social activism—almost as if one could bring about the kingdom by signing up enough voters. This was the Christian right in the eighties and nineties, and the Christian left in the sixties and seventies.

5) *Debate the culture*. Take a missionary approach on the assumption that we live and work in a post-Christian culture.

Avery Dulles simplifies the possible relationships between culture and Christianity by reducing them to three models— the confrontation model, the synthesis model and the transformation model. Similarly, communications researcher James McDonnell breaks down the approaches into rejection, accommodation and assimilation.

All of these overlapping typologies are instructive, especially when considered together. For together they offer a comprehensive continuum of options, running from a gnostic total rejection of the culture at one extreme to an idolatrous total identification with the culture at the other. (Quentin Schultze, a student of Chrisianity and electronic culture, applies the gnosticism-idolatry schema to television critics and advocates.) A chart at the end of this chapter puts this in a graphic format.

Most thinkers on church and culture plant themselves firmly at some point along this spectrum. In the earliest centuries of the church, for example, the Fourth Gospel (John 17: 11-14) and the famous *Letter to Diognetus* were in the middle with a stance that Christians should be "in the world though not of the world," in that famous phrase from *Diognetus*. John and the writer of *Diognetus* heard God's call to Jeremiah to promote the welfare of the city (Jeremiah 29:7). In our day, social critic Malcolm Muggeridge argues from the separatist end in *Christ and the Media* that Jesus would have spurned the offer of a prime-time television broadcast as Satan's fourth temptation. Similarly, author Michael L. Budde contends in *The (Magic) Kingdom of God* that any hope "to restore the vitality of the churches using the tools of the culture industries seems doomed to failure or frustration." At the antipodes from Budde and Muggeridge lie the megachurches, which adopt the media technologies of the electronic age with great enthusiasm and apparently few doubts.

I contend that the church should be at different places on the continuum at different times, in response to the times and the circumstances. The challenge is to discern where she is supposed to be at any particular moment. And the standard for determining that isn't success (what works), but faithfulness. The church's engagement or disengagement with the mass-mediated culture has to be faithful to God's truth in all its forms. This includes being faithful to:

> the Word of God (in Scripture, Tradition and the living Christ);
> the church (the community, the Body of Christ);
> the uniqueness of the human person (made in the image and likeness of God);
> the text (message) and the context (circumstances or location).

Being faithful may mean, for example, not only comforting but also challenging—as Jesus challenged the rich young man when he told him to sell everything (Matthew 19:21). Faithfulness may also mean not meeting the congregation's felt needs which have been created by the mass media, but rather their real needs. To the Samaritan woman who wanted well water, Jesus gave instead the living water she really needed (John 4:7-14).

Surprisingly, the Old Order Amish offer a good model for negotiating the church's relationships with media. Contrary to the common perception, the Amish don't reject all technology. Technophile writer Howard Rheingold, in an article called "Look Who's Talking" in the January 1999 issue of *Wired*, calls them "techno-selectives." They use kerosene lamps and propane refrigerators. Some even accept the telephone for calling doctors and suppliers, but they require that phones be used communally and not in the home. An Amish workshop owner explained to Rheingold that his community fears assimilating the "dangerous ideas that 'progress' and new technologies are usually beneficial, that individuality is a precious value, that the goal of life is to 'get ahead.' This mind-set, not specific technologies, is what the Amish most object to." In my terms, they strive to be faithful to their tradition, to their community, to their context. Now the Amish debate whether to use cell phones, as many are doing already under the rationale that they help hold the community together. Rheingold calls the controversy "part of the continuum of determining whether a particular technology belongs in Amish life."

Where the church should be along the spectrum from rejection to acceptance of the media culture—or any aspect of it—is a continuing negotiation. The answer changes with new technologies and new contexts. But let's look at some indicative examples of how I believe the faithfulness criterion should be applied in parish ministry. Because they're points on a continuum, the three categories into which I've divided the possible responses aren't as sharply defined as the headings suggest.

Disengage

This is the most negative approach, and not the usual one. But at times the church *should* reject the high-technology and high-technique expectations of the mass-mediated culture. Sunday is one of those times, though in practice the opposite is true: The liturgy is a primary zone of accommodation to the culture in many Protestant and Catholic churches. Movie screens in the sanctuary, professional singers in the choirs, and variety-show trappings turn the Sunday service into one more entertainment option. And as Generation Xer Sarah E. Hinlicky notes with an almost audible sniff in a *First Things* magazine column, "we can find better entertainment elsewhere."

What the church should offer is not *entertaining* liturgy but *good* liturgy. Faithful Christian liturgy is ritual, ancient but ever new, that transports one to a different reality and a participation in the life of Christ. It forms and transforms the Christian believer. That's the source of excitement in good liturgy, not the constant three-ring circus stimulation that we find in some congregations. A friend of mine attended a wedding at a megachurch in which dry ice was used to create an atmosphere for the bride's walk down the aisle. "It was interesting," my friend said, "but it wasn't holy." Liturgy should be holy.

Instead of vibrating with the cultural norm of all-sound all the time, the church should also offer a deeper silence in the liturgy and in church life generally, encouraging her members to "be still, and know that I am God" (Psalm 46) in faithfulness to Scripture. Free of background noise, unplugged and unwired, one can better hear God's tiny whisper, that still small voice that Elijah heard (1 Kings 19). Silence isn't aural, visual, entertaining, novel, stimulating, commercial or controllable. It's better—the mute harmony of our deepest encounter with the true self and with God, the top of communication. It's more important in a worship service than professional singers. And yet, it's hard to find in our parishes. Silent prayer or meditation before Mass is next to impossible amidst the chatter in the pews.

In the sacred space in which the service is to happen, a movie screen stands as an intrusion. The biggest object in the sanctuary should be the altar or, arguably, the font—certainly not a screen. Screens are inescapable almost everywhere else in our lives. The church should offer sanctuary from that, a place where the only images are paintings, statues, and stained glass—non-electronic media that don't move or speak (except to our hearts). Audiovisual media imitate life with recorded sound and images composed of photons of light. We should never mix that with liturgy. For liturgy is real life, made with flesh and blood, grapes and wheat, candles and incense. It's incarnational; it's human. It isn't imitation and it isn't show business.

The church should also reject technological media as substitutes for human contact when that contact is possible. Wendell Berry, the Kentucky poet and farmer, wisely cautions in an essay that a new technology "should not replace or disrupt anything good that already exists, and this includes family and community relationships." Writing in *Harvard Business Review*, psychiatrist Edward M. Hallowell argues the need for what he calls *the human moment*, "an authentic psychological encounter that can happen only when two people share the same physical space." This is a psychiatrist confirming what Christians should already know, that community and the highest level of communication demand co-presence—embodiment.

That's why communion can't be offered online or confessions heard over the telephone. Sacraments involve all of our senses in ritual encounter with God. We can't have that without a body, and the body of believers, physically present. For Christians faithful to the uniqueness of the human person, the body isn't just a container of the soul, as the leader of the Heaven's Gate cult called it; it's an integral part of the person. Hence, the National Conference of Catholic Bishops/United States Catholic Conference Committee on the Liturgy, in a June 1999 statement on "The Sacraments via Electronic Communication," wrote: "The celebration of the sacraments requires the physical and geographic presence of both the gathered faithful and the bishop, priest, deacon or other presiding minister." Why? "As regular participants in video conferences report, electronic communication is incapable of transmitting the full range of human communication. As the ancient maxim *ubi epicopus, ibi ecclesia* [where the bishop is, there is the church] implies, true 'presence' is physical and geographical by definition."

Challenge and Change

While disengagement is opting out of mass media culture, the first level of engagement with media is to confront media-formed cultural expectations with a radical alternative. It has elements of both rejecting media (in that it doesn't buy into all of its assumptions) and accepting (in that it acknowledges the media culture instead of ignoring it). This should be the "default option" or the norm for Catholic Christians, just as disengagement is for Old Order Amish.

For example, a strong emphasis on the liturgical year, with its periods of waiting at Advent and Lent, fundamentally challenges a world geared to immediacy and instant gratification. Advent challenges commercial Christmas, the most media-hyped holiday, by marking off the season with weeks of preparation—not shopping days. Lent challenges Easter season sales with a period of reflection and self-denial. (We could say in the same vein that silence challenges the aural culture as well as rejecting it. Or we could say that Advent and Lent disengage the culture. These are close points on the continuum.)

The church should confront the entire commercial success model of church that church-growth advocate George Barna embraces when he writes in *The Frog in the Kettle: What Christians Need to Know About Life in the Year 2000*: "If we hope to include people in the life of the Church, we must provide appealing and high quality activities that can successfully compete for people's time, attention and resources. Church programs should include more entertainment-related activities." The faithful Hebrew prophets, who didn't take their cues from the marketplace or cultural norms, offer a better paradigm: As Douglas D. Webster points out in *Selling Jesus: What's Wrong with Marketing the Church*, "They resisted the religious powers' accommodating efforts to reassure people that their greedy consumption, entertaining worship and striving for success met with God's approval."

Adopt

The church can never be synonymous with the culture and still be the church. But, Muggeridge and Budde notwithstanding, the church can use electronic media without becoming captive to the culture industries. The church can use electronic media to subvert the negative elements of electronic culture just as Jesus used parables to subvert the oral culture and post-modern writers use books to subvert the print culture.

Terry Mattingly asks, "Would Paul ignore the media?" Pope John Paul II answers "no" when he calls the mass media "the modern equivalents of the Areopagus" in his 1990 encyclical *Redemptoris Missio* (37c). In his apostolic exhortation *Ecclesia in America*, following the Synod for America in 1997, the pope writes: "Contemporary reality demands a capacity to learn the language, nature and characteristics of mass media. Using the media correctly can lead to a genuine inculturation of the Gospel" (72). The pope himself is a worldwide media figure who has made sophisticated, effective and faithful use of television and the Internet. An earlier pope, Paul VI, declares in *Evangelii Nuntiandi* (1975): "The Church would feel guilty before the Lord if she did not utilize these powerful means that human skill is daily rendering more perfect" (45).

But how can she do so faithfully?

The first and most available way is at the consumer level. All of the ministries cited above as zones of confrontation can also be zones of adoption for popular media production when appropriate—preaching, sacramental preparation, catechesis. All of these and other ministries can use commercially produced films, television programs and Web sites in appropriate ways to reach people with the Good News. We'll see how in later chapters.

With adequate resources of skilled people and money, the church can also "make media." Only the personal witness of human beings can really evangelize. But mass media can pre-evangelize, or prepare the way for the gospel, if the church uses media in an evangelistic way, not merely to market. Marketing is filling identified needs; it's finding a niche and targeting a market audience. Evangelization, by contrast, is an invitation into the life of Christ, an offer of companionship on the journey of faith. The church can and should make that offer through faithful use of "the modern Areopagus" in all its forms:

Aural. Christian radio, featuring a heavy component of music, is one of the most popular formats in radio. The music, whether ancient hymns of the church or "contemporary Christian," can uplift the spirit and confirm the faith of committed Christians. It may even pre-evangelize. Music is a good use of radio for the church, but it's not the only one. Less common formats seldom explored by Catholic radio stations have great potential. Modern parables in the form of radio dramas could challenge the complacent and convert the unconverted, as Jesus' parables did. Call-in programs would let seekers ask the questions that bedevil their hearts, as so many of Jesus' disciples did. Family Theater Productions, a Catholic enterprise, brilliantly combined the two approaches with a soap opera in Spanish, each episode followed by a call-in program to discuss moral issues raised in the storyline.

Visual. The most common types of religious presentations on television are televangelism and the TV Mass, both problematic for the church. The weakness of televangelism isn't that it's *on* television but that it's *like* television. The format, offering the excitement of variety rather than the familiarity of ritual, is more likely to resemble a talk show than a liturgy. An evangelist-centered program designed to build an audience and generate contributions is inevitably entertaining, simplistic, validating, stimulating, and comforting. That's what holds a television audience. It's also idolatrous. Televangelism reaffirms adherents of the star, but doesn't evangelize. It's not how the church, called to "make disciples [for Jesus Christ] of all nations" (Matthew 28:19), should use television.

Televised liturgy presents a different concern. The TV Mass evangelizes, but it isn't church. Remember, the U.S. bishops' Committee on the Liturgy said that liturgical celebrations "depend upon the *physical presence* of the gathered faithful." Liturgists who argue that sacraments are to be celebrated in the presence of persons, not watched on television, are right. The TV Mass is no substitute for physical presence at the liturgy in the viewer's own faith community. It's a picture of the Mass; it's not the Mass, as TV Mass veteran Rev. Miles O'Brien Riley likes to say.

But no one has ever pretended anything else. A televised

Mass never satisfies the Catholic's grave obligation to participate in the Sunday Eucharist if physically able. It was never intended to. Rather, the TV Mass is a pastoral concession and outreach to shut-ins who *aren't* physically able to participate— it's connection, not community. (Community exists in the communion bread taken to the sick.) On that basis the TV Mass is an appropriate use of television for the church, but it's not the best use.

What, then, *is* the church's best use of television? The church should use television to do what television does best— tell stories. Stories evangelize, whether they are the stories of people we know who were touched by the hand of God, the lives of the saints, or the struggles of holy ones in our own day such as Oscar Romero and Dorothy Day. This could take the form of dramas, documentaries, news stories, or interview programs. They all tell stories, just as Jesus did and just as TV commercials do. But television works most effectively when it *shows* what it's trying to convey. So does evangelization. Jesus knew this when he answered the question about his identity by telling inquirers to report to John what they had *seen* and *heard* (Luke 7:22).

Television has the capacity to "reach beyond the choir," to capture the attention, the imagination and the hearts of channel surfers who aren't consciously seeking a religious experience. That makes it a perfect medium for pre-evangelization, preparing one for the gospel. But when the goal is teaching or reaffirmation, there's another way to use video called "group media." This is showing a video to members of the particular audience for whom it's intended, often small groups at a time in a ministry setting. You could think of it as "narrowcasting" instead of broadcasting. Your diocesan media center probably has hundreds of instructional tapes for this kind of use, such as the *Catholic Update Video* series from St. Anthony Messenger Press.

Or maybe your diocese has done its own video that would have great relevance for your local church. The Archdiocese of Cincinnati, for example, produced a video with Archbishop Daniel E. Pilarczyk called *Keeping the Lord's Day: An Invitation to Joy.* It's a video version of the Archbishop's series of articles about why Sunday worship and Sunday rest are important. The video is divided into four parts, each ending with a series of questions to help study groups and prayer groups reflect on and share the meaning of Sunday in their lives. In Indiana, the state's Catholic Conference authorized the showing of a ten-minute video, *Talking About the Death Penalty,* at all Masses in conjunction with the church's Jubilee Day for Prisoners on July 9, 2000. A companion brochure highlighted the most important points the video makes about the church's death penalty teaching. The goal of programs like these is faith formation. A video alone can't work that formation, but the active participation and personal witness of its viewers can.

Digital. In the early days of fax machines, someone who wanted to send a fax would call the prospective recipient and say, "Do you have a fax number?" Now that same person calls and says, *"What's* your fax number?" It's just a given that businesses—and most parishes—have a fax machine. Fax machines are digital and no one questions their use in the church. We aren't quite there yet with cyberspace in the church, but we soon will be. Journalists and prospective parishioners will say, "What's your Web address?" instead of "Do you have Web site?" We'll discuss in chapter nine how to build your Web site on the proper foundation, picking the right goal and letting it determine your content.

Radio, television, non-broadcast videos, and Web pages can all be ways for the church to use electronic media faithfully, but only if they are tools of pre-evangelization and confirmation—not marketing.

For Reflection

- *How do the mass media fit into the life of your parish or other ministry site now? How do you think that should change?*

- *What has been the most memorable liturgy in your life? Why? What would make liturgy better in your parish?*

- *How does your parish distinguish different liturgical seasons—for example: Advent, Christmas, Lent, ordinary time?*

CHRIST AND CULTURE: A CONTINUUM OF APPROACHES

	Disengage	Engage / Challenge and change	Accommodation	Assimilation	Adopt
Quentin J. Schultze	Gnosticism				
James McDonnell	Rejection		Accommodation	Assimilation	
Terry Mattingly	Burn the Culture	Change Culture	Debate Culture	Baptize Culture	Photocopy Culture
H. Richard Niebuhr	Christ Against Culture (Radicals, Exclusivists)	Christ Transforming Culture (Conversionists)	Christ & Culture In Paradox (Dualists)	Christ Above Culture (Synthesists)	Christ of Culture (Cultural Christians)
Avery Dulles		Transformation	Confrontation	Synthesis	
Malcolm Muggeridge	Television is fourth temptation of Christ				
Michael L. Budde	Eschew tools of culture industries				
The Gospel of John (John 17:11-14)		In the world, not of it			
Letter to Diognetus		In the world, not of it			

FOUR

A Media Fast—Lent and Beyond

Before we look at how to use the mass media in ministry, let's consider how to not use them in our daily lives—the disengagement response at the individual level. Tuning out from media for a while is an excellent way to prepare yourself for re-engaging media thereafter with more intentionality and discernment. It's a little like the fast before communion, a "virtual fast" from electronic media.

I urge you to take a day once or twice a week to get "unplugged" as much as possible in the spirit of Jesus withdrawing to the desert to renew himself. Leave the computer unbooted, the video games unplayed, the beeper or cellular phone in a drawer for the day (unless your job demands otherwise). Proclaim for yourself what Cardinal Carlo Martini calls a "day of silence."

You can do this any time, but the season of Lent—during which fasting is a traditional practice along with prayer and almsgiving—would be particularly appropriate, especially if you want to encourage the whole parish to participate.

Six Spiritual Reasons

I'm not talking about "giving up" television or the Internet as a sacrifice, although that might be a good discipline. Nor do I mean turning off the tube or radio in disgust over the programming content. This isn't a participation in National TV-Turnoff Week. (But at least one parish, Our Lady of Good Counsel in Plymouth, Michigan, successfully participated in TV Turnoff Week as a form of Lenten fasting.)

No, my notion of fasting from electronic media is something more spiritual. What I suggest is not so much a giving up as an opening up—to God, God's world and God's people. There are at least six spiritual reasons for anyone (not just parish ministers) to go on a virtual fast, all of which are liberating rather than sacrificing:

To Create Silence in our Lives. As we noted in chapter two, electronic culture is aural. Every home, office and car has a radio. Our computers talk to us. Cell phones ring everywhere. Television is aural, too, even though we think of it as primarily visual. In fact, TV is the always-present background noise of daily life for many people. Watching or listening to television is what they do when they "aren't doing anything." Turning on the TV is the first thing they do when they enter a room, and turning it off is the last thing they do at night before they go to bed. Even in many poor countries this is the habit. I once sat in a small apartment in Havana with a host family who left a television on, in the kitchen where we were sitting, during an entire evening of conversation.

In 1 Kings 19, the Bible gives us the story of the prophet Elijah standing on the mountain waiting for God. And the surprising thing is that God doesn't come in the strong wind, or in the earthquake, or in the fire, but in a tiny whispering sound—"a still, small voice" (12), some translations say. God still speaks to us in whispers. But how can we hear when our ears (and hearts) are tuned to the sound of electronic culture? As the world gets ever noisier, we have an even greater need for the silence that has always been part of the spiritual life.

To Create Time in our Lives. Pope John Paul II seemed to have this in mind when he said during a Lenten blessing several years ago: "A certain 'fasting' in this area [media] can be helpful, in order to give more time to reflection and prayer and to cultivate human relationships."

Relationships, whether with friends and family, with our inner selves or with God, require an investment of time. The lack of time may be the most common complaint in America today. Where does all that time go? Electronic media steal a lot of it. How much time do you spend watching, listening, interacting with electronic media each week? How much time do you spend in prayer? How much time do you spend with family and friends? The U.S. Census Bureau figures on media use in 1996 added up to more than eight hours spent on TV, radio, recorded music, plus another 44 minutes on print media. That doesn't leave a lot of waking time for building solid relationships.

And the Census Bureau tabulation didn't even consider computers, which rival TV as the most-used appliance in some homes. Computers can help relationships by bringing family and friends together through E-mail. They can connect one with spiritual insights available on the Internet in hundreds of religious World Wide Web sites. But cyberchat can also steal family time—and has even destroyed marriages.

To Open Contemplative Space in our Lives. Saint Clare of Assisi, the patron saint of television, wrote a prayer in which she urged us to "transform your entire being into the image of the Godhead itself through contemplation." In other words (those of Psalm 46), "Be still, and know that I am God."

A contemplative focuses on one thing at a time instead of being bombarded with sensations, with busyness, or even with images. The monk Thomas Merton, in an essay in his book *New Seeds of Contemplation* called "The Pure Heart," warned about the danger of television preventing that: "Certainly it would seem that TV could become a kind of unnatural surrogate for contemplation: a completely inert subjection to vulgar images, a descent to sub-natural passivity rather than an ascent to a supremely active passivity in understanding and love. It would seem that television should be used with extreme care and discrimination by anyone who might hope to take the interior life seriously."

More recently, the comic strip "Betty" made the same point. In the first panel, Betty's son walks by her while she is sitting in a lotus position. "What's with Mom?" the son asks his father. "Your mother is meditating—it's an eastern way of putting oneself into a trancelike state," Dad explains. In the final panel, the son says "I prefer the Western way" and the father says "Ditto" as they ensconce themselves in front of the television in the trancelike pose of the couch-potato.

Television, the Internet, the radio and even cell phones can be spiritual junk food. They fill us up with sounds and images that may keep us from being lonely—and also allow us to avoid facing ourselves.

To Compose our Hearts for God. "Christian Tradition has retained three major expressions of prayer: vocal, meditative, and contemplative," notes *The Catechism of the Catholic Church.* "They have one basic trait in common: composure of heart."

Electronic media also compose our hearts, but usually not for God. This is where content counts, not just the amount of time spent on media. The late spiritual writer Henri Nouwen, discussing television and prayer in his book *Gracias: A Latin American Journal,* noted the negative impact of TV images on his thoughts, feelings and actions. "These imposed images actually make us into the world which they represent, a world of hatred, violence, lust, greed, manipulation, and oppression," he decided. We lose our identity in these images, Nouwen said. When we get rid of them, prayer and contemplation can lead us to our true identity. Cardinal Hickey, in his column asking Catholics of his archdiocese to turn off their cell phones during Mass, appropriately urged his readers to "pay much more attention to the original form of wireless communication, namely prayer."

Electronic media have the capacity to present truth, beauty and knowledge. And sometimes they do. But if the best programs in the electronic media don't appeal to lust, greed, pride, sloth, and gluttony, the commercials surrounding them do.

Sister Nancy Lee Smith of Monroe, Mich., is an icon painter. The discipline of the iconographer involves prayer and fasting before painting. As a Type II diabetic, she can't fast from food. Instead, she fasts from television. "I realized I can't bring beauty out of my home if I'm bringing junk into it," she told Catholic News Service.

To Improve our Mental and Physical Health. The shock-and-titillate formula of much television and radio content, from talk shows to the nightly news, may be as harmful to our mental and physical health as to our spiritual health. Popular self-help guru Dr. Andrew Weil thinks so. He suggests occasionally taking a "news fast" to get away from all the negativity of the "If it bleeds, it leads" school of journalism that is so prevalent in TV newsrooms.

What will you miss if you don't pay attention to "the news" for a few days? Not much that will really make a difference in your life. Nature writer Bill McKibben spent a day in the woods away from the media culture. With the help of friends, he recorded everything available on television that same day on the nation's largest cable system. He wrote a book, *The Age of Missing Information*, comparing the two experiences—a day in the woods and a day watching television. He concludes that he learned more that was useful and real from his day of reflection in the woods.

To Make Ourselves More Aware of the Huge Role of Media in our Lives. The process of trying to take a sabbath from electronic media for a while will make it apparent just how hard that is—how much a part of the fabric of our lives television, radio, computers and cell phones have become. One of my seminary students used the analogy of a house: You get a different view from the outside than you do from inside; and sometimes it looks a lot bigger from the outside. That's a good perspective to have as you prepare to look at media with ministry in mind, and at ministry with media in mind.

Getting Ready

You might start with a pre-Lenten exercise to drive home the point. For a week or so before going on your media fast, keep a log of what you watch on television, what you hear on the radio, what you see on signs and billboards while you're driving. Then reflect on the experience in your journal: How much of all that media improved me, spiritually or intellectually? How much of it entertained me, which is a legitimate function of media? How much was just background noise or, worse, an addictive time killer? What would I like to do with my life that I don't have time to do?

You'll notice, if you're attentive enough, that the catchphrases and icons of TV and films aren't confined to electronic distribution channels. They also circulate on bumper stickers, billboards, signs, casual conversations ("Is that your final answer?") and clothing with corporate logos and Hollywood images. They come at us unbidden as we go down the street or—especially—walk through a mall. And they become three-dimensional as licensed characters at theme parks and restaurant playgrounds.

In Full Retreat

So how is it possible to avoid all that? You could go into a monastery or follow Bill McKibben into the woods. That might not be a bad way to launch your fast, with a self-directed silent retreat or day of reflection. But if you're going to stick with this you'll probably have to create your days of silence by staying at home and turning off your television, radio and even the computer.

Then fill the newly created quiet with praying, walking in the woods, dining with friends, writing long-overdue letters, playing board games (ones not inspired by TV shows or movies) with loved ones, reading to younger children, or in some other way nourishing your soul. Do whatever you wrote in your journal that you didn't have time to do. Listen for the still, small voice of God. "Yes, we need to return to ourselves if we want to rediscover ourselves," Pope John Paul said in encouraging a Lenten media fast. "At stake is not just our spiritual life but a sense of personal, family balance."

You might take up your journal again, this time to note what you've learned about yourself, your family, the world created by God, and the world of people during your media fast. Ask and answer questions such as: Am I really missing anything important during this fast? Do I miss electronic media anyway? Am I a calmer person when I'm unplugged? Do I relate any differently to other people? Am I doing things that are a more valuable use of my time? To what degree are the effects of electronic media still with me even though I'm on sabbatical from participating in it?

To step away from the electronic media for a while isn't to tune them out, but to tone them down in terms of their role in our lives. Turning on the TV shouldn't be an automatic activity or a ritual but a decision. The decision isn't just *what* to watch or listen to, but *whether*. Fasting from television and other electronic media and their commercial offspring can remind you of that while bringing you closer to God and God's works, including other people. And that can stay with you long after Lent gives way to the joy of Easter.

Beyond Lent, Beyond Human Billboards

Media fasting doesn't have to be a Lenten-only activity. You could make it a once-a-week practice all year long. How about taking a sabbath from electronic media every Sunday? Also, set a daily or weekly limit on how much time you spend with television and the Internet. Unplug the speaker on your computer. Turn off your cell phone, your television, your computer when you're talking with someone. Go on a silent retreat.

And there's another way to carry the spirit of the media fast beyond Lent: You could make it a spiritual practice to boycott media-inspired and media-hyped clothing. Buy T-shirts and sweatshirts without words on them, for instance. Everybody agrees there's too much advertising on television, on radio and in the Sunday newspaper. But what about on our bodies? That should be even more offensive, spiritually and morally.

Americans willingly spend millions of dollars each year on T-shirts, sweatshirts, caps and other apparel that turn themselves into walking billboards for name-brand products, designers, companies, characters and sports teams. Been there, done that, bought the T-shirt. Columnist Leslie Savan is right to say we're all living "the sponsored life." We're sort of reverse prostitutes—instead of selling our bodies to advertisers, we pay them for the privilege of advertising for them.

It's hard not to. When I set out to buy a baseball cap a couple of years ago, it took a major search to find one that wouldn't mark me as "a Nike guy" or a "Cincinnati Reds guy." I never did find a truly generic cap. I settled for one that simply says the name of my state, "Ohio." I don't like it much, but at least I'm not shilling for a profit-making corporation whenever I put it on.

Logo-laden apparel is so commonplace that everyone could get the joke when the comic "Mixed Media" showed a couple watching the pope on television with Nike's swoosh emblazoned across his chest. "OK . . . Nike's gone too far," the man says. But a student in my wife's seventh grade religion class went even further. As part of a class assignment to design a new church, he drew a sanctuary sponsored by Nike. The company's familiar corporate logo adorned the priest's vestments, the altar, the steps, the ambo, the cushioned seats, the "flat escalator so you don't have to walk down the aisle," the tabernacle—even the communion wafers. The swoosh trumped the cross.

Corporate icons have replaced religious ones in a broader sense as well. They don't just brand the product; they also brand the user or the wearer—as "with it" and well off. But Christians are supposed to be branded by the sign of the cross, traced on our foreheads at baptism. Sure, the cross is still popular as jewelry, but it has lost a lot of market share, not to mention religious significance.

"You Are What You Drink" is more than a Diet Coke slogan. It reflects perfectly the reigning mindset in Western cultures that equates a person with his or her product preferences. Today a designer label doesn't just say who the designer is; it says who (and what) the wearer is. You may be clothed with Calvin Klein, or Homer Simpson, in exactly the same sense that Saint Paul says the baptized are clothed with Christ (Galatians 3:27).

A comic strip called "Rhymes with Orange" captured the soul of various labels perfectly—and the *zeitgeist* of our age as well—with a series of panels called "Signature Looks." Calvin Klein (the label but also the customer) was classed as "slick and sexual," Tommy Hilfiger as "rich and sporty," and Donna Karan as "hip and urban." The last panel, "the rest of us," showed a bug-eyed woman gripping a cup of java above the legend "sleepy and disheveled." Message: The clothes make the woman. This is a culture in which "having" is elevated over "being," which Pope John Paul II condemns in *Centesimus Annus* (36).

Overstated? I don't think so. A friend of mine overheard a woman at a suburban food court expressing dissatisfaction at a potential combination of resources involving her Catholic parish and another. "The kids who go to that school can't even afford Nikes," the woman sniffed. And a non-traditional student in a college course I teach recalled a boyfriend who suddenly stared at her and asked, with some dismay and distress, "Is that a generic sweater you're wearing?"

There is a kind of idolatry here. God forbids us to make idols out of created images (Exodus 20:4). A tribe of primitive natives does just that with a Coke bottle that drops out of the sky in the film *The Gods Must Be Crazy*. So does anyone who remakes himself/herself or anyone else—any human being created in the image and likeness of God—into the avatar of a corporate product (such as MacIntosh), identity (Coke), logo (the swoosh), designer (Ralph Lauren), character (Winnie-the-Pooh), or team (Chicago Bulls).

Am I saying there's something morally wrong with wearing spirit wear for your daughter's high school basketball team? Not unless it becomes the definition of your identity and a measure of your worth—which is possible. Absent that seduction, what you're advertising makes all the difference.

Ethics in Advertising, the 1997 document from the Pontifical Council for Social Communications, teaches that advertisers "are morally responsible for what they seek to move people to do" (14). It follows, then, that some share of that responsibility devolves to consumers who become walking billboards for immoral products or companies with immoral practices.

Camel and Marlboro, for example, offered entire catalogs of branded products, many of which have nothing to do with smoking. In 1995, the tobacco industry spent $665 million on merchandise giveaways and catalog sales, according to Federal Trade Commission records. (Children who sport clothing and gear emblazoned with tobacco logos are four times more likely to smoke than other children, said a study published in *The Archives of Pediatric and Adolescent Medicine* in 1997.) The beer companies (one of the biggest of which is owned by a tobacco company) also put their brand names on T-shirts and caps. I saw this kind of apparel on the streets of Havana, presumably sent to Cuba by better-off relatives in the United States. The irony of advertising harmful luxuries in a nation where so many need so much was inescapable.

Wearing clothing without designer labels, corporate logos or licensed characters isn't easy, but it is doable. Just Do It. You'll be opting out of at least one negative of media culture—not only for yourself, but for anyone who reads your clothing.

A Ministry of Absence

This may be great personal spirituality, but is it ministry?
　It can be.
　First of all, when you turn off the sound and take off the labels you bring a bit of aural and visual silence with you wherever you go. To a tiny degree you are helping create

silence, real or metaphorical, for others.

Second, you're a quiet example to those others by how you live and how you don't live your life.

Third, your own experience gives you a great vantage point from which to urge an electronic media fast and a walking billboard boycott in your parish.

Finally, retreating from mass media for a time will help make you much more discerning when you return to radio, TV, movies and the Internet. You will be better grounded to "read the signs of the times" in the media and carry that into your ministry.

For Reflection

■ *What is the "background music" of your life? How do you feel without it?*

■ *Do you feel the need to be constantly connected through computers and cell phones? And do you feel uncomfortable when you're "unplugged"?*

■ *What wardrobe items with advertising do you own? Why do you own them?*

FIVE

Reading the Signs of the Times

Avoiding the self-branding that happens when you wear commercial apparel is something you can do all the time. But fasting from electronic media is something you shouldn't.

In discussing the work of inculturation, the *General Directory for Catechesis* says "the Christian community must discern, on the one hand, which riches to 'take' up as compatible with the faith; on the other, it must seek to 'purify' and 'transform' those criteria, modes of thought and lifestyles which are contrary to the Kingdom of God." We can't do that without some awareness of the mass media, for media and culture are inseparably linked.

I usually ask my students to discuss in groups this reflection question: "If Jesus had a television set in his home, how do you think he would use it?" There are always some students who say "He wouldn't." But Jesus ate with both Pharisees and sinners; he was immersed in all elements of the culture of his day. He also criticized the religious leaders of his day for not being able to "judge the signs of the times" (Matthew 16:1-3). Drawing on that, the Second Vatican Council's *Gaudium et Spes* (4) says the church has the responsibility to read the signs of the time and interpret them in the light of the gospel. Today, the place to find the signposts of our culture is in the mass media, especially television and other electronic media. If you're going to minister effectively in a media age, you have to be familiar with the output of the culture industries. That doesn't mean spending hours a day in front of a screen, whether computer or television. But it does mean you should see at least some of the most talked-about movies and TV shows, read some of the best-selling books, and surf the Internet from time to time. Only then can you both challenge the mass media and use them in your ministry, as appropriate.

I divide the signs of the times into four categories. Maybe you could think of more, but mine are:

Print, including books, magazines, newspapers, newsletters, tattoos, greeting cards, packaging (cereal boxes are my favorites), and especially comic strips. The hot topics of our culture always find their way into the comics. So do the most important visual symbols. Look at today's comics page in your newspaper. How many strips include panels with a TV screen or a computer screen? That's a sign of how much these technologies "screen" our lives.

Electronic, incorporating aural, visual and digital media—television and the VCR, remote control, movies, radios, fax machines, computers, photocopies, audiotapes, video games, automated teller machines, telephones (especially cellular), beepers and answering machines.

Representational, by which I mean toys, games, dolls and even Halloween costumes—our playthings that send serious messages about what we value and especially how we value persons. What are the most popular Halloween costumes or Christmas gifts this year? What values are imbedded in these items?

Institutional, such as hospitals, jails, malls, schools, churches. While these aren't mass media in that sense the term is usually used, they do convey a message. Does your community have more jails or hospitals? Are your churches or your athletic fields more crowded on Sundays? Do your children spend more of their after-school hours in malls, gyms, or libraries?

All of these signs tells us important things about our culture if we pay attention. And as we saw in chapter one, the print, electronic and representational media are all intertwined through the culture industries matrix. But the electronic media are the signs we live with the most, as you know if you've tried to live without them in a virtual fast. G.K. Chesterton, the late British man of letters, once wrote in his newspaper column that "man's basic assumptions and everlasting energies are to be found in penny dreadfuls and halfpenny novelettes." The position that cheap literature held in Chesterton's day as a social barometer has been largely taken over by TV and movies.

Just as Jesus criticized those who are unaware of their culture, he also deplored those who are uncritical in their approach—those who look but don't see, and hear but don't listen or understand (Matthew 13:13). We need to read the signs of the times critically.

In this spirit, the church recognizes that media literacy— the skills to understand, analyze, evaluate, and produce media—should be incorporated into the curricula of all seminaries and church-run schools. The Vatican documents *Inter Mirfica* (1963), *Communio et Progressio* (1971) and *Aetatis Novae* (1992) all call for media education. *The Guide to the Training of Future Priests Concerning the Instruments of Social Communication* (1986) specifically requires mass media to be a part of seminary training. The Protestant community, in the National Council of Churches' 1995 statement on "The Churches' Role in Media Education and Communication Advocacy," also calls for media education in families, churches, and schools of theology.

Media literacy proponents broadly agree on several core concepts that anyone who hopes to engage the media critically must master. They state them in as few as four propositions and as many as eight. Probably the most widely used

list of these principles of media literacy is one developed by
the Center for Media Literacy. It consists of five key points:

All Media Are Constructions, a Particular View of Reality.
Everything presented by media is necessarily edited to tell a
story, whether that story is a commercial or a news account.
Nothing is or can be "raw reality." That's why this is a mass-
mediated culture. Even C-SPAN cable channel, which appears
to be unedited, comes to us through filters—the decision of
what to broadcast and what to skip. This isn't as obvious to
most people as it may seem. As a character in Michael
Crichton's 1996 novel *Airframe* says: "The image is the reality, and by comparison day-to-day life seems to lack excitement. So now day-to-day life is false, and the media image is
true. Sometimes I look around my living room, and the most
real thing in the room is the television."

Media Use Unique "Languages" or Techniques. This is *how*
they construct reality. The "language" differs with the
medium. Print media may use words, photos and charts to
communicate, for example. Audiovisual media employ a
range of sounds and camera techniques. The Internet pulls it
all together—text, video, audio. Sound is a bigger part of the
language of video productions than we notice most of the
time. When I showed a group of deacon students a video clip
without words or musical background, one of them assumed
the VCR was broken. We're also so used to television that we
forget the flat screen is a language for communicating a three-
dimensional reality. I once talked with a Catholic priest from
Africa who told me that the residents of his small village
couldn't "see" television—they didn't understand the language of two dimensions.

Audiences Make Their Own Meanings. The traditional
Source=>Message=>Channel=>Receiver model of communications, which assumes that the receiver gets precisely the
message sent, is too simplistic. The signal belongs to the trans-
mitter, but the meaning belongs to the receiver. No media pro-

duction has an objective meaning that is exactly the same for all its consumers. The audiences read it, and read *into* it, in the light of their own worldview influenced by their age, sex, class, religion and politics. A satirical movie that offends some Catholics, for example, may raise questions that provoke a faith experience in others. So communication theorists generally have abandoned the "transmission model" or "transportation model" of communication, so called because it looks at media as delivery systems. In its place many communicators have adopted the "ritual theory," which says that media mediate culture and relationships.

Media Have Commercial Interests. As we saw in chapter one, they're in business to make money. They do so by selling the media product (video tapes, movie tickets), by selling advertising with the product, and/or by selling products (toys, games, dolls) based on the product. To generate profits in any of these ways, the programming has to be designed to capture an audience. It's worth stressing that journalism is no exception to the profit motive. Although reporters and editors tend to think of themselves as an underpaid priestly class, the news business is highly profitable for the companies that employ journalists. In television, the news used to be considered a loss leader; it's now a money maker. Even public broadcasting has commercial interests in the form of corporate underwriters, station members who contribute money to keep their favorite shows on the air, and the sale of products related to PBS and NPR programs.

Media Have Embedded Values and Points of View. Since everything is edited, everything has an editor. No editor is value-free, nor is any media production. What do TV programs and movies say is important? Sexuality, youth, beauty and health, success, happiness, simple solutions, power and especially the possession and consumption of material goods. Mostly that, but not only that. Every television season also brings individual episodes or even entire series that lift up gospel values and virtues such as faith, hope, love, redemption, forgiveness and conversion.

Understanding these five core concepts of media literacy can help pastoral ministers and their parishioners understand what media do and how they do it. But media literacy isn't enough if we're to engage the mass media as Christians. We need to read the mass media through *two* lenses and hear through *two* ears—one of media literacy and one of the Christian gospel. The principles of media literacy tell us how media are constructed. The principles of the gospel tell us how to construct our lives. Using both enables us to reflect theologically on the stories of the mass media through the story of Jesus. That's essential for engaging the mass media critically in preaching and in Christian formation. There's a checklist at the end of this chapter to help you, and an example of how to apply it to a popular movie.

You can put a film clip, a music video, or a sitcom segment into tension with any relevant Scriptural text. But there are several New Testament passages that provide sure touchstones to the moral compass of Jesus. The Sermon on the Mount in Matthew 5 has been called a handbook for Christian living, and the Beatitudes in that sermon (5:3-12) tell us who Jesus considers blessed or happy. The great judgment scene in Matthew 25:35-40 describes the deeds of a righteous person—virtue in action. And the Magnificat, Mary's magnificent hymn (Luke 1:46-55), summarizes the teaching of Jesus that God finds favor with the powerless and the poor. Does the latest episode of TV's hottest sitcom or this week's top music video deliver the same message? Or is it a sign of the times that our culture is far from the kingdom of heaven?

For Reflection

- *Do you think Jesus would own a TV set? If so, how would he use it?*

- *How does the constructed reality of the mass media compare with the reality of Jesus?*

- *What does a Christian see in the world that the news reports and the dramas or comedies miss?*

A MEDIA CHECKLIST FOR CRITICAL REFLECTION

This instrument is designed to help the reader/viewer engage mass media with a critical viewpoint and a Christian perspective. It can be applied to anything from a commercial to a movie, a comic strip to a novel.

Title: _____

Value	Message Presented	Message of Tradition/Scripture
Religion (God, Church)		
Human person (worth/value of life, stereotypes, sexual relationships)		
Material goods (brand names, poverty, wealth)		
Violence		
Other		

See next page for Sample Checklist.

SAMPLE CHECKLIST

Title: *STAR WARS Episode I: The Phantom Menace*

Value	Message Presented	Message of Tradition/Scripture
Religion (God, Church)	One supernatural Force contains both good and evil. The Chosen One, predicted to bring balance to the Force, has no human father.	Star Wars dualism seems similar to the Manichaeism, which taught that good and evil are equal eternal forces. Jesus, the Messiah, was conceived by Holy Spirit and born of a virgin.
Human person (worth/value of life, stereotypes, sexual relationships)	Droids at times seem human. Deaths are often treated humorously.	Human beings are created in the image and likeness of God, special in all creation. Jesus came so that we might have life, and have it in abundance.
Material goods (brand names, poverty, wealth)	A slave is the Chosen One.	God has thrown down the rulers from their thrones but lifted up the lowly (Luke 1:52).
Violence	The queen will not condone a course of action that will lead to war. In practice, violence is the answer to the problem in most situations in the movie.	Jesus says, "Blessed are the peacemakers" (Matthew 5:9).
Other	A Jedi knight says to "concentrate on the moment."	Jesus says not to worry about tomorrow (Matthew 6:34).

Six

Tuning In the Parish
to Media Literacy

The last chapter introduced or reintroduced you to media literacy and the gospel as two lenses for answering Christ's call—and the church's—to read the signs of the times in our culture. This chapter is about how to carry that double-lensed perspective into the parish.

My favorite commercial for illustrating values of the mass media is the popular Nissan ad from a few years ago. An Indiana Jones look-alike doll comes to life in the mouth of a dinosaur, slides down a rope, climbs into a toy red Nissan, tears across the room, and finally comes to a screeching halt in front of a magnificent doll house. When he whistles, a Barbie doll clone appears on an upper floor. The hero merely nods toward the car. She smiles. A split second later she's sliding down a fire pole, dressed in a slinky cocktail dress. Another male doll, reminiscent of Barbie's beau Ken, appears on the porch of the dollhouse with a sad smile on his face and a tear in his eye.

When I showed this commercial to the entire student body of my parish grade school, two or three grades at a time, I asked—as I always do—what its message was. A third or fourth grade girl correctly replied: "If you are a guy and you drive a Nissan you get an awesome girl." After my talk, which was a forty-five-minute crash course in media literacy, one student summarized it in writing this way: "Don't let your TV get smart. When you're TV smart, you don't let TV push you around."

The kids got it.

But how many of their parents get it?

Almost all of the students I talked to that day said they had computers, though ours is not an especially wealthy parish; most had at least three TV sets in the family, some as many as seven; many watched MTV, even among the first- and second-graders; and almost all had seen any movie I mentioned. Kids are saturated in mass media, much of it conveying values antithetical to the gospel. Their parents, with the help of church leaders and religious educators, should encourage them to put their faith and the mass media into tension. That means learning to ask themselves, for example: Do the values of this action-adventure movie reflect or conflict with the values of Matthew 5-7 and Matthew 25? In other words, young people need to understand that there's no such thing as "just entertainment" free of values messages. They need Christian-oriented media literacy.

But a parish that wants to help families teach their children to be media literate can't just work with the children. It's the parents who let their first-graders watch MTV (if only by their absence), parents who buy the computers and multiple TV sets, parents who take their younger kids to movies or rent them. So parents and other adults in the parish also need to become "TV-smart"—and movie-smart and Internet-smart—because they aren't now. They need to be in order to help their children. Whatever message the parish or school conveys won't have much impact if it isn't reinforced at home.

Introducing media literacy to the parish should start with presentations to parish staff, teachers, parents, and other adults (including parents whose children are not in the parish school). These could be free-standing programs or linked to something else, such as a parish staff meeting, a Parent-Teacher Organization meeting, a faith enrichment program in Lent or Advent. When you make a presentation that's open to the entire parish, make a special effort to get volunteers from all your parish ministries to participate. After the topic has become a parish talking point, introduce ongoing programs for children (including those in the parish school of religion) and incorporate aspects of media literacy as a regular component in parish ministries where appropriate.

The St. Mary School Parent Media Awareness Group at St. Mary parish in Cincinnati brought in a regionally known media literacy speaker and high school teacher to present a program for parents on the effects of TV on children. That's a good way to do it, but not the only way. Excellent materials are available to enable you or a volunteer to introduce various groups in the parish to media literacy without an outside speaker.

At the top of the list for parishes, even though it is several years old, is *Catholic Connections to Media Literacy*. This is a complete kit sponsored by the Catholic Communications Campaign (of the U.S. Conference of Catholic Bishops/United States Catholic Conference) and produced by the Center for Media Literacy in cooperation with the National Catholic Educational Association. It's not only a great introduction to media literacy with a Catholic Christian vantage point, but a tool box for teaching the subject to a range of age groups and ministry settings. The kit includes a twenty-minute video that introduces the core concepts of media literacy, a leader's guide and handout masters for fifteen basic learning modules adaptable to both youth and adult groups, and a sourcebook for media literacy education in Catholic schools and parishes. The sourcebook, *Forming Values in the Media Age*, contains sample two-hour sessions for junior high, senior high, late adolescent, adult faith formation, peace and justice groups, marriage preparation and family life, teachers and parish leaders.

I built my first talks on gospel-centered media literacy around snippets from the *Challenging the Image Culture* video in the *Catholic Connections* kit and *The Writing on the Wall*, a video from Columbia Theological Seminary's *Signs of the Times* series. I added more video clips, plus handouts, to illustrate specific points as I reworked the presentation for different audiences. If you have a passion for the subject, you too should be able to develop your own presentation using materials from a variety of sources.

And if you want to zero in on a particularly troublesome aspect of media, such as sexual images, violence, or commercialism, there are plenty of more focused materials to help you. The Center for Media Literacy, in addition to being a one-stop source for books and videos on media literacy from a myriad of sources, also has produced kits on parenting in a TV age, tobacco and alcohol advertising, values in the news, sexism in the media, and violence in the media. Many of these, and more that you can find listed on the center's Web site, may be available at your diocesan media center.

A major presentation on media literacy from a gospel perspective should cover:

The Definition of Media Literacy: Media literacy, remember, is the ability to understand, analyze, evaluate and produce media.

The Principles of Media Literacy. *Challenging the Image Culture* and the five-minute *Taking Charge of Your TV* video from the Family and Community Critical Viewing Project each present these basics, although in slightly different versions from the list in the previous chapter. Other chapters of this book will help you explain the links among commercialism (advertising as the heart of mass media), media values (which are commercial values), and sex and violence in media (to draw audiences to advertisers).

A Gospel Values Paradigm Against Which to Measure Media Values. I like to suggest Matthew 5:3-12, Matthew 25:35-40, and Luke 1:46-55, as I did in chapter five. You may find other passages helpful. Adapt my media checklist as a tool for making the comparison.

Positive and Negative Aspects of Television, Movies, Music and the Internet in the Light of the Gospel. Generate your own list of the pluses and minuses of each, but only use it to fall back on. Encourage your audience members to give their opinions first. They probably won't be shy.

Tips on How to Manage Television in the Family. For parents, this is the most practical media issue. They need help. At the end of this chapter is a collection of suggestions that represent the common wisdom of media literacy activists. In addition to using these ideas as part of a presentation, you could make them into a bulletin insert or weekly bulletin series (one suggestion per week) and put them on your Web page.

All of this is a lot to pack into one presentation for any of the groups you want to reach. You don't have to. You can spread it out over several sessions. I've done media literacy in five sessions for teachers, two sessions for anyone in the parish who was interested, one long session for parish staff, one short session for grade school students. (At the end of this chapter is an updated version of the outline for my presentation to the students. Notice that I use the five core concepts of media literacy without ever calling them that. I also invite the young students to compare values of the media to the values of Jesus.)

You might want to create a committee either to find an expert to talk about each of several media literacy topics or to divide up the topics and have each member make one presentation. It could be a limited run over a concentrated period, such as four Wednesdays in Advent, or it could be a major effort once a year during Lent—this year focusing on television, next year on the Internet, etc. You won't run out of topics.

Members of the St. Mary School Parent Media Awareness Committee present a monthly series of classes on media for grades K-2. (Media literacy is incorporated into the curriculum on the archdiocesan level for the higher grades.) Drawing on materials from media literacy Web sites and the archdiocesan media center, the volunteers devote three classes to commercialism, three classes to heroes, villains and negative behaviors (violence), and two classes to images. To pull parents into the process and have them reinforce the messages of the day, the students go home with a printed note outlining the lesson and some questions to ask about it. Here's one:

The Media Mentor visited your child's class today.

Today we talked about:
What you see isn't always what you get.
Some tricks used to "dress up" commercials.
Media-wise: We see through the disguise.

Ask your child:
What are some of the tricks used in commercials?
Why do people in commercials usually seem happy?
Whether they think the tricks are good or bad.
If they've ever felt tricked by a commercial.

This is a great approach for reaching young kids and their parents. You should also incorporate gospel-centered media literacy into many of your other family ministries on an ongoing basis. For example:

Marriage Preparation and Marriage Support

As a couple approaches marriage, the parish should encourage them to confront the views of marriage and family that are prevalent in the mass media and how they have affected the couple's expectations. How do the problems of TV families relate to real life? How do their answers relate to real life? What does TV teach you to expect out of marriage? How does that compare to what your experience teaches you to expect out of marriage? Engaged couples should discuss the role that television, computers and cell phones have played in their families and how they will be a part of the family their marriage will create. Is TV going to be a companion at every meal? How many TVs will you have in your home? Where will they be? The biggest mistake we made in dealing with TV in our family was to put the set in our basement family room. It seemed like a good idea to isolate TV from the rest of the house. In practice, it isolated our kids from my spouse and me when they went down there to watch TV (by permission only) while we read or worked around the house.

The comic strip "Hi and Lois" once had the next door neighbor showing off a family portrait—husband, wife and television. "It's like part of the family!" the neighbor explained in the last panel. As we've seen, TV is a family member that can sometimes divide the rest of the family as they fight over the remote or watch different sets in separate rooms. Father Bill Rose of the Diocese of Toledo discussed the problem as part of a marriage enrichment night. He talked about how movies, television, the Internet and cell phones can be barriers to marital communications.

Baptism Preparation

Any baptism class that is more than just the mechanics of the baptism day must deal with how we pass on faith to our children. Mass media may help or hinder that, but they will always be a factor. The baptism preparation class is another opportunity to encourage parents to think about how media are used in their home. How will you use TV with your children when they are small? What TV-watching limits will you set for your children? How will you confront the values that mass media bring into your home and compare/contrast them to the values of the gospel? (For families bringing an older child to be baptized or with other children already in the home, these are practical present-tense rather than theoretical future-tense questions.)

For Reflection

- *Who has the energy to bring media literacy to your parish? Who has the knowledge? Who has the heart?*

- *What resistence do you expect? How will you overcome it?*

- *Who are the local or regional experts you can call in?*

Some Guidelines for Managing TV in Your Home

Kick the TV habit. Make television watching an intentional activity, not an automatic one. Decide to watch particular programs, not television. Plan your viewing in advance. Don't turn on the tube as soon as you enter a room. Don't channel surf.

Create your own library of quality commercial-free videos for occasional watching. Either buy them or edit out commercials as you tape them off of television.

Set a weekly or daily limit on how much television your children may watch, even good TV. It's not just the quality of television that matters, but also the quantity. Setting the limit over a longer time frame (week vs. day) allows some flexibility for tradeoffs—no TV tonight so that we can watch a movie tomorrow night.

Limit your own TV watching. Christians witness by example. Children follow what you do and not what you say.

Don't watch TV during meals. Talk to each other instead.

Don't use TV as a babysitter. This is a hard one because it's so tempting. But would you pacify your child with drugs the way you want to pacify her with television? Even educational TV programs or videos shouldn't be used this way.

Don't increase TV time as a reward for good behavior. Too much TV is too much TV even when a child has been good.

Turn off the television when a guest enters. That person is more important than any television program.

Go on a media fast for Lent. (Remember those six good spiritual reasons in chapter four.)

Have only one television set in the home. No child should have a TV in his or her own room where it separates the child from other family members. With one TV, family members learn to make the tradeoffs and choices involved in negotiating which program we watch tonight.

Make it clear to your children what your criteria are for choosing programs. Light entertainment is a perfectly valid reason for watching a sitcom; crude humor that debases the human person is a perfectly good reason for *not* watching a sitcom.

Watch TV together as a family. Talk about each program and its values—before (if you know enough about it), during, and afterwards. Are those values the values of the gospel? Do the decisions the characters make about sex, violence and money conform to the gospel or do they conform to this age? Discuss what the characters should do in the next few minutes and compare that to what they probably will do. Talk during the commercials.

Let TV be a starting point. Read the novel that was the basis of the show or movie. Read more about the history and the geography behind the story. If the setting attracts you, plan a vacation there if you can.

Write to the network, local station manager and commercial sponsors of shows that you feel strongly about, either to praise or to criticize their approach to religion, race, sexuality and gender issues.

Remember that the best parental control device for television isn't the V-chip; it's the parents.

SCHOOL PRESENTATION OUTLINE
SIX FACTS ABOUT MEDIA

I. **What you see or read isn't reality, it's someone's version of reality. Even in a photograph, you never see the whole picture. Someone always decides what to put in, what to leave out.**

Newspaper or TV news story
   1. reporters try to be fair, but no one can present every per-

spective of even the smallest event
2. there's always an editing process—it often begins in the mind of a reporter before an editor gets involved

Commercials
1. every problem is solved in thirty seconds if you just buy the right product; that's not really the way the world usually works
2. sometimes the products aren't even like they are in real life—Ask: Have you ever been disappointed by a toy after seeing a commercial for it?
3. a good way to see how commercials are different from real life is to ask yourself whether you would actually say the words that kids say on TV commercials

TV shows
1. men outnumber women 3 to 1 on TV; the real world is 51 percent female
2 there are fewer non-white people on TV than in real life
3. there is more crime on TV than in real life
4. Ask: Are the people you know like people on TV?

II. Media have their own special languages that they use to communicate and make us feel the way they want us to feel.

Movies and TV
1. camera angles
2. special effects
3. music (show example)

Newspapers and books
1. words
2. charts
3. graphs
4. photographs

III. Audiences make meaning. In other words, different people may understand the same show differently.

**What you think is the most important point of a story
may be completely opposite what the person in the
next seat gets out of it because you have different
backgrounds, different ideas.** This means you don't
have to be a couch potato mentally, just accepting
everything you see on TV or in the movies you can
ask:

1. "Is this true?"
2. "What would Jesus do?"

**IV. Media are in business to make money from you and
your parents.**

Movies make money many ways

   1. ticket sales in theaters
   2. rental and sales of VCR tapes
   3. sales of all kinds of products that come from movies

     a. computer games and video games, especially action
       movies (most new toys are based on movies)
     b. action figures and dolls. Ask: What are your favorite
       action figures and dolls?
       (1) show *Toy Story 2* promotional dolls
       (2) show *X-Men* products
       (3) show *Star Wars* figures
     c. movie makers are paid to use particular brands of
       products in movies, such as Nike or Coke (show
       current example)

Ask: *TV doesn't charge you to watch a particular program, so how
do they make money on TV shows?*

   1. primarily commercials

     a. most people think that advertising brings you
       programs because it pays for the cost; but really,
       programs bring you advertising
     b. always remember that the only reason TV
       programming exists is so commercials can be
       wrapped around it

      c. in order to make the most money from advertising, TV needs to get the largest possible audience—so that's its goal, not the best possible programs

  2. some TV programs are all commercials

     a. *Ask:* Do any of you watch MTV? All of the videos on MTV are commercials for the albums

     b. *Ask:* Do any of you watch the *Pokemon* TV show? It's a show created to sell the cards and other products (show Pokemon commercial)

  3. TV is also paid for showing particular brands of products, just as the movies are, which is another form of commercial

  4. newspapers, radio and online computer services also make money from advertising

Ask: *Did know that* you *can also be a commercial?*

    That's what happens when you wear a jacket or a sweatshirt or shoes with a big logo on it. You become a walking billboard advertising that product—but instead of getting paid, you pay for the clothing

V. Media communicate values and points of view: they *inform* us, tell us stuff; but they also *form* us, make us who we are.

  1. *Ask:* What are values?

     a. what is important to us

     b. our principles that tell us what is right

  2. the values of commercial media are mostly the values of commercials

     a. many commercials and programs communicate that you aren't cool unless:

       (1) you have certain things

         (a) certain clothes

         (b) a certain scent

         (c) a certain car (show car commercial)

    (2) you look a certain way
      (a) pretty (Barbie) or handsome
      (b) slim
      (c) strong (G.I. Joe)
      (d) perfect—no handicaps
3. many programs communicate that human life isn't worth very much because violence is the only way they show to solve problems

The values of Jesus are completely different; Jesus said:
1. "Blessed are the poor in spirit, for theirs in the kingdom of heaven." (not rich)
2. "Blessed are the meek, for they will inherit the land." (not strong)
3. "Blessed are the merciful, for they will be shown mercy." (not vengeful)
4. "Blessed are the peacemakers, for they will be called children of God." (not violent)

VI. All kinds of media can be both bad and good.

1. *Ask:* What can be bad about TV, movies, music, computers?
    a. they can communicate bad values
    b. they care about your money, not about you
    c. if you spend too much time with them, they keep you from doing other things—(ask them to name some)
      (1) playing with friends
      (2) reading
      (3) homework

Am I saying that mass media are always bad? No.
1. media inform and entertain
2. those are both good things as long as we remember those first five important points

What you see or read isn't reality; it's someone's version of reality
1. media have their own special languages that they use

to communicate and make us feel the way they want
us to
2. audiences make their own meaning; you don't have to
   accept everything you see and hear
3. media are in business to make money from you and
   your parents
4. media communicate values and points of view

SEVEN

Preaching the Word
in an Image Culture

All Christians are called to proclaim the word with their lives. Preachers also have the gift and call to proclaim the word in words. The formal preaching moment brings with it both advantages and challenges in this multimedia culture. The chief advantage is that the preacher in such a situation is the focus of attention by an audience primed and ready to listen.

The biggest challenge is the disposition of the preacher's listeners. Yes, they're expecting to hear the word. But in our culture, what Neil Postman calls "the Age of Show Business," they're also expecting to be entertained. They have short attention spans. They are used to seeing as well as hearing.

Robert P. Waznak, S.S., in an article called "Preaching Gospel in a Video Culture," says that the homily's primary goal is "to spark the imagination of listeners so that they will read the signs of the times in the light of the alternative world of the gospel." I suggest that to do this a homily should both reflect the electronic culture in style and challenge it in substance.

That means, first of all, to tell stories. That's what Jesus did, and that's what electronic media do. The Bible is mostly stories. All forms and genres of mass media tell stories. Sitcoms, movies, news stories, advertising—they all tell stories. Many writers on media literacy have called TV commercials the parables of our age. Preachers have the opportunity to create their own parables to compete with, for example, the Parable of the Beer that Fills Without Bloating. Like Jesus, they can use stories to challenge their listeners instead of giving instant solutions like the thirty-second parables on the TV screen.

Preachers can also appropriate stories. They can draw from anywhere—from the Bible, from the stained glass windows in the church (a visual and rich source), from today's news, or from the movies. But it's the stories taken from the electronic media that most touch people where they live today. One, not bound by the Common Lectionary, preached a seven-week sermon series called "Everything I Needed to Know I Learned From Andy Griffith." He preceded each talk with a video clip from the classic TV series and illustrated his points with a PowerPoint presentation, both projected on a screen in the sanctuary. While I don't think the screen in the sanctuary is appropriate, the concept of drawing from the mythology of television and movies to make a Scriptural point certainly is. Perhaps the point is even stronger when the show or film is current and much discussed.

Fulfilled in Your Hearing: The Homily in the Sunday Assembly, issued in 1982 by the Bishops' Committee on Priestly Life and Ministry of the National Conference of Catholic Bishops, makes this point: "Dramatic presentations that deal sensitively with significant human issues can provide a wealth of material for our reflection and our preaching, both in its content and in its form." *Dead Man Walking* and *Cry, the Beloved Country* are about forgiveness, for example. *Places in the Heart* is about the communion of saints. *Field of Dreams* is about being called by name. *Life is Beautiful* is about hope. The journal *Visual Parables*, edited by Presbyterian minister Edward McNulty, includes in each issue a feature called "Lectionary

Links," offering thematic and theological connections between the readings in the Common Lectionary and popular films. Songs also tell stories. A preacher can use the words and story lines of popular music with great impact.

In retelling the stories of our culture, the homilist can also put them in tension with the Lectionary reading. Are the values the same or different? Whose values do we live by, those of the gospel or those of Hollywood? You don't only have to talk about movies or shows that illustrate the gospel. One thing you should be careful about, though, is potential minefields in movies you cite. A movie that carries a powerful and positive message may be great for adults yet unsuitable for children. You don't want to give such a film a *carte blanche* endorsement in your homily, so be sure to add the appropriate caveats.

Another danger with storytelling in a homily is that you can get so wrapped up in the story that it becomes a distraction from your point. Be careful not to veer "off message," as the political spin doctors put it. In his aptly named book *Preaching Better: Practical Suggestions for Homilists*, Bishop Kenneth Untener stresses several times the importance of sticking to one core thought and developing it well. And that core thought should flow from the Scripture readings, Untener says, not something that you want to say with the Scriptures as the occasion for saying it.

Story isn't everything, of course. In crafting the homily, don't forget the importance of images. A homily is oral, which grants it a hearing in this secondary oral culture, but it also should be visual. That doesn't require a projection screen in the sanctuary. There are already a lot of images in the worship space to draw on for inspiration and illustration—stained glass, statues, icons, paintings, crucifixes, stations of the cross in whatever artistic medium.

And a preacher can, and should, create images with words. Be concrete, not theoretical; inductive, not propositional. Remember, Jesus invited the disciples to come and see for themselves (John 1:39). And instead of answering whether he was the one to come, he told the disciples of John to report back what they had seen and heard (Luke 7:22). So use what our elementary school teachers called "picture words." If you think you write concretely, Bishop Untener recommends going over a written transcript of one of your homilies with two different colored felt tip markers—"one color for picture words and another for those that aren't." The results may surprise you. "Only when I saw the transcripts of my own homilies was I convinced that so many words were not concrete," the bishop writes. Preaching professor Thomas H. Troeger suggests in his book *Ten Strategies for Preaching a MultiMedia Culture* actually writing the homily as a movie script, with lots of detail to create a cinemagraphic image in the listener's mind.

A homily isn't a lecture, exposition or catechesis. And it isn't an article, although many print-influenced preachers seem to miss that point. The homiletic style of today's preacher should be suitable to the secondary oral culture that's emerging rather than the linear print culture that's passing away. That means the homily doesn't have to proceed from point A to B to C in logical order like the pages of a book. It doesn't always have to be a sustained narrative. It can jump around a bit—like a movie, a TV show or a visit to the Internet. You could offer a series of images, verbal portraits of people, or vignettes around a central theme. Or in rare circumstances you could break out completely from traditional format with a dialogue homily, playing on the interactivity of electronic media.

Being appropriate to secondary oral culture also means, like it or not, that a homily should be short. "The 30-second commercial, the 10-second sound bite, the three-minute news report, the 10-minute entertainment slot are serious challenges to the long-winded homily," Waznak writes. Making just one point, not three, will help. Several years ago a book called *The One-Minute Manager* sparked a rash of "one-minute" books. I'm not advocating a one-minute homily, although Father Greg Friedman, O.F.M., comes close with his "Sunday Soundbite" feature on www.AmericanCatholic.org during Lent and Advent. But it might be a useful exercise to ask yourself how you would convey the message of your homily in a one-minute commercial.

For Reflection

■ *Revisit the last homily or reflection you presented or heard. Does it tell a story? Could the descriptions be more concrete? Could the narrative be more cinemagraphic?*

■ *What is the key word in the Gospel for next Sunday? What popular movie, TV show, or commercial either supports the Gospel on that word or conveys a different message?*

■ *How would you write a homily for next week if you had to do it as a thirty-second radio spot or a sixty-second TV commercial?*

EIGHT

Using Media in
Christian Formation

A good reading of the signs of the times should inform all ministries in a parish or other faith community, not just preaching. And while I don't think it's appropriate to bring the screen into the sanctuary to augment a homily, video clips can have a place—an important one—in Christian formation. I'm using that phrase "Christian formation" in a broad sense because formation is what all ministry is about: not just taking care of people, but forming them.

Media often form their users in ways contrary to the gospel. But they can also be used to bring the gospel to human hearts. In fact, religious educator Robert Sarno argues that faith and audiovisual media are a perfect fit. Both, he points out, transcend words, speaking in symbols. And both appeal to the right side of the brain, the seat of creation and intuition, rather than the left side, the center of logic.

In this chapter we'll look at a grab bag of ministries and methods of using media, starting with probably the most obvious form of Christian formation—catechesis.

In *Sharing the Light of Faith: National Catechetical Directory for Catholics of the United States*, the U.S. Catholic bishops acknowledge that media are part of the lived experience of candidates and catechumens that should be addressed in catechesis. They write that ". . . catechists should learn how to take media into account as a crucial part of the cultural background and experience of those being catechized; how to use media in catechesis; and how to help their students understand and evaluate media in the light of religious values." In the same spirit, *The General Directory for Catechesis* calls media "essential for evangelization and catechesis."

We've already noted how the media, especially electronic media, have helped to create and sustain our audiovisual culture and how that has affected the church. By calling for taking media into account as part of the cultural background of the catechized, the U.S. bishops are asking catechists to read the signs of the times in the mass media as all ministers should do: Read several of the best-selling books. Watch the top-rated TV programs at least occasionally. See the most popular movies.

Catechists also should reflect, along with candidates and catechumens, on how the forms and characteristics of the mass media affect the Christian life. For example: How does "channel surfing," the quick switch to something new when interest wanes, undercut commitment as a value in our daily lives? How does the emphasis on the urgent and the new in the audiovisual culture affect a catechumen's readiness to accept 2,000-year-old Good News? How does the "quick fix" of the TV commercial which solves every problem in thirty seconds affect the way our culture views redemptive suffering?

When the bishops write about using media in catechesis, they may mean using videos, slides or PowerPoint as teaching tools or religious videos as mentioned in chapter three. All of those have their place. But using the popular media of the culture is more promising. Movies and TV programs, read through the prism of the gospel, can offer parables of our age. They are stories we share, stories that most people know.

Works of overtly religious intention—such as television's "Touched by an Angel" and "Seventh Heaven" or films such as *Romero* and *Entertaining Angels: The Dorothy Day Story*—obviously can be sources of catechetical material. But so can many other shows and films. Within just four days of each other, two NBC dramas showed a police officer using a rosary to pray for his dying father ("Homicide") and a President of the United States receiving the Sacrament of Reconciliation in the Oval Office after failing to spare the life of a condemned man ("The West Wing"). When I showed a clip of the latter in my seminary class, even my most anti-TV students recognized its power. My wife once worked with an eighth grade catechumen whose only admitted exposure to Scripture was a "Rugrats" episode based on the story of Moses. That was a rather meager religious background, but it was a start.

An older film that remains powerful, the Academy Award winning *Places in the Heart*, provides a wonderful illustration of the communion of saints. The camera pans slowly across each communicant at a Protestant communion service until it surprisingly shows the heroine passing communion to her husband—who was killed at the beginning of the film. He smiles at her, then passes the cup to the black man who shot him and was himself later lynched by a mob. A number of other characters who had died earlier in the movie also share communion. This final scene closes the movie with a forceful visual statement that the communion of saints reaches beyond the bounds of death.

Television shows and movies don't even have to have any obviously religious scenes to be helpful for catechesis. I once used a scene in the Christmas film *The Santa Clause* to make a faith point. When a junior elf remarks to Bernard, the chief elf, that "Seeing is believing," Bernard replies, "Believing is seeing." So it is with most of Jesus' miracles, I noted—faith precedes miracles instead of miracles producing faith. To illustrate the Christian virtue of hope, you couldn't do any better than the Italian film *Life is Beautiful*. Without any religious references, the Jewish lead character brings hope out of despair in a concentration camp.

These are just a few examples of how I've used secular productions in catechesis. You'll find your own by watching with the eyes and listening with the ears of faith. It's not necessary to show a large section of a movie or TV show. In fact, it's more effective to set up the clip with the appropriate explanation and then show just the most powerful two or three minutes. You can pause it, rewind it, ask questions about it. The video isn't the teaching or the teacher; it's the tool.

I also liked using comic strips in catechesis. As *Communio et Progressio* says, "Comics and illustrated stories are not to be despised." The irony and humor of a comic often makes a theological or moral point memorable—and relevant. They're also cinemagraphic in the way they tell stories. And every day's newspaper yields a fresh bounty of material.

"Frank and Ernest" frequently deals with creation themes and the Ten Commandments. In one comic, Moses stands with the Tablets in his hand saying, "Wait a minute—this isn't one of those 'Take responsibility for your own actions' deals is it?" I used that in a catechetical session on sin and free will. A "Marmaduke" panel shows the big dog with his mouth on a pastor's arm in a gesture of guidance. The pastor protests, "I appreciate the thought, Marmaduke, but I already have a shepherd." We talked about that Good Shepherd. Robert L. Short wrote a whole book on *The Gospel According to Peanuts* in 1965. Other comics often having religious themes include "B.C.," "The Family Circus" and "Dennis the Menace." Whatever comics your newspaper has, read them in the spirit of theological reflection and you'll find much for catechetical use.

Taking into account the media culture, using the media, helping parishioners understand and evaluate media—the three dimensions that *Sharing the Light of Faith* calls for—aren't desirable only in catechesis. Let's look at how they can apply to other parish ministries as well:

Adult Faith Formation

Parishes struggle to provide continuing faith formation for fully initiated Catholic adults. They offer RENEW, Bible study and small faith communities. But relatively few have tapped into the transformative power of film. More should. How about a film festival for Lent or Advent, for example? It doesn't take a film expert to lead a discussion, just someone attuned to reading movies theologically. Watching movies together in the parish hall, and reflecting on them together afterwards, isn't as contradictory to my call for a Lenten media fast as it may seem. A six-week moratorium on channel surfing and video watching one or more days a week could prepare your parishioners for a more intentional and deeper experience of a film festival each Wednesday night (or whenever).

What movies would be appropriate? You could start with a movie about Jesus and move from there into Jesus figures, offering a journey from the most concrete to the most abstract telling of the Jesus story. The line-up might be something like this: *Jesus of Nazareth* (last hour or so), *Romero, Entertaining Angels, Dead Man Walking, Babette's Feast.* Or you could choose movies that illustrate such religious themes as faith, hope, love, conversion (transformation), justice, forgiveness, vocation, resurrection, redemption, grace, Eucharist/thanksgiving, sin and reconciliation. Challenge participants to compare what the film has to say about the discussion theme to the generally accepted viewpoint of our culture and the teaching of Scripture and Sacred Tradition.

At the last session of the film festival you could pass out copies of Cardinal Roger Mahony's excellent pastoral letter "Film Makers, Film Viewers: Their Challenges and Opportunities." It opens up a series of religious questions that can be applied to any film for reflection, not just overtly religious ones.

Another approach would be a Lenten media retreat that challenges the predominant values of the mass media from a social justice perspective. Lutheran pastor Bill Gafkjen put together a retreat on "TV and the Christian Faith" for students at Penn State, where he was then a campus minister. After showing participants a TV commercial for a loan company, he broke the big group down into smaller groups and asked them to identify the myths, ideologies and values embedded in it. They shared these insights with the large group, then broke into the smaller groups again to compare how these myths, ideologies and values compare to the gospel. Another approach might be to give three small groups different tasks: Identify the prevailing values of TV shows (Group 1), TV commercials (Group 2), and the gospel (Group 3). My guess is that Groups 1 and 2 would have similar reports, while Group 3 would stand as a sign of contradiction.

Smaller faith groups could use electronic media as well. One Web site (www.barneyfife.com) points the way with a series of Bible study lesson plans based on "The Andy Griffith Show." You could create something similar with a currently popular TV program that often deals with values issues.

The Jesus Video Project takes a different approach to using media for faith formation, one that doesn't seem to invite theological reflection. Bill Bright, founder of Campus Crusade for Christ, in 1974 commissioned a direct-to-video movie about the life of Jesus, based on the Gospel of Luke. Sponsors mail the video in bulk to all the homes in a target zip code (often offending non-Christians who receive it). It's a laudable, interdenominational effort, but there's a big problem with the approach: Media don't evangelize; people do. Mass-mailing the video as one would a sample of a new soap—without personal contact, personal witness, and a forum for reflection on the film and what it says about Jesus in the viewer's life—is unlikely to bring recipients to a relationship with the Lord. Watching and discussing videos as a group, by contrast, provides for human interaction and a sense of the church as an interpretive community. It's an interactive process, communal rather than individualistic.

Ideas for Confirmation Classes and Youth Ministry

Put together a film festival or a youth retreat using movies. Sister Rose Pacatte, FSP, director of the Pauline Center for Media Studies in Boston, encourages Parish Movie (or Video) Nights for young adults, showing and discussing movies as she has done in many parishes. She breaks it down into an eight-step process:

Identify a popular feature film that tells a story well, with the dignity of the human person at the center (e.g., *Grand Canyon, Princess Caraboo, Dead Poet's Society, Dying Young, The Spitfire Grill, Beyond Rangoon, The Killing Fields, Ulee's Gold, Koyla, Cinema Pardisio, Central Station* for starters.)

Obtain a non-theatrical license from the Motion Picture Licensing Corp., (800) 462-8855 or fax (310) 822-4400. This company provides an annual low cost license on behalf of more than forty studios and other copyright holders. They also do a quick turnaround on requests.

Create a simple poster for the parish church, the parish hall, the church bulletin noting date, time, title of the film, refreshments and time for dialogue and fellowship after the viewing.

Reserve the space and equipment. Prepare the space and make sure the equipment is working.

Preview the film yourself before the showing.

Prepare a simple handout with questions to think about. When the film finishes, have a break with refreshments, then resume with five minutes to reflect on the questions.

If you are concerned about the dialogue getting off to a good start, pass out small pieces of paper before the viewing with the names of the characters on them. Ask participants to view the film through the eyes of the character. When the dialogue begins, ask: "What was the role of your character in the film? Or what part did your character play in the conflict or its resolution?"

Conclude with a moment of silence, opportunity for spontaneous prayer and the Our Father.

At the end of this chapter is an example of another way to go. It's a three-session retreat for junior high students. Each session, lasting about an hour, looks at scenes from a different movie about growing up and invites a gospel-based response. I wrote the retreat with my wife, Ann Brauer Andriacco, who still uses it successfully with seventh graders in a Catholic school. It originally appeared in REEL TO REAL magazine. You might want to create a similar retreat using movies currently popular with the age group to which you are ministering.

Prayer

Petitions that take into account the media are appropriate any time, but the Pontifical Council for Social Communications each year offers Prayers of the Faithful suitable for Masses on the annual World Communications Day. In 2000, the Council's World Communications Day petitions included:

That believers who work in the world of social communications may be creative and fearless in proclaiming the gospel through these media, let us pray to the Lord.

That families, enlightened by the Holy Spirit, may teach their children wisely to choose the true and constructive messages from among the many offered by the media, let us pray to the Lord.

That parish communities and the entire Church may inspire professional vocations to bear witness to Christ in the media, let us pray to the Lord.

That the investors in and owners of the means of social communications may understand the good they can do their public by spreading the gospel message and promoting its dissemination, let us pray to the Lord.

That those who work in Church media may carry out their work with enthusiasm and hope, let us pray to the Lord.

With these petitions as examples and inspiration, your parish Worship Commission could regularly produce petitions on behalf of those who work in the media and those who are affected by the media.

Sister Pacatte created a wonderfully innovative "Praying the News" novena for the nine days leading up to Christmas. The service for each evening consists of a Biblical theme appropriate to Advent, a "To Think About" quotation from a church document on media, ten minutes to watch the evening news (live or taped) or look at newspaper/magazine/Web news, a period of silent reflection, a round of shared insights, spontaneous prayers and petitions, and closing group prayer. Participants view or read the news, reflect on it and pray about it through the lens of the theme or the opening quotation.

The Parish or Faith Community at Large

There are a number of less targeted ways media-conscious pastors, pastoral associates or directors of religious formation can reflect the mass-mediated environment in which they minister. Here are a few ideas to start you thinking:

Form (or turn your parish library into) a parish media center that includes worthwhile videos. Be sure to include the VeggieTales videos for preschool kids, who love these animated vegetables that retell Bible stories and take on serious questions like "Where is God When I'm Scared?"

Carry brief movie reviews in your parish bulletin. Or simply print on a regular basis the phone number of the Catholic Communications Campaign's movie hotline, (800) 311-4CCC. The service, updated every Friday, provides capsule reviews of six currently popular movies and a recommended "Family Video of the Week."

Hold a family movie night once a month at the parish hall.
One parish does this, regularly drawing thirty to sixty
families with young children. Parents take turns hosting.
The host family picks the movie.

For Reflection

- *What is your current favorite film or TV show? How could
you incorporate a segment from it into your ministry?*

- *What problems will you face in using media in your
ministry—logistics, equipment, resistence by co-workers or
congregants?*

- *How is Jesus Lord of your television? How is Jesus Lord of
your pocketbook (or is the commercial culture)?*

A YOUTH RETREAT

SESSION ONE: *Jack*

*And can any of you by worrying add a single hour to
your span of life? If then you are not able to do so small
a thing as that, why do you worry about the rest?* (Luke
12:25-26)

Theme: Christ calls us to a child-like simplicity that includes
freedom from worry and faith in God to provide the
necessities of life.

Purpose: Youth will learn that maturation does not mean
giving up the childlike qualities of healthy adults such
as curiosity, innocence, openness, vulnerability and
freedom from fear.

Background: Jack (1996) is 133 minutes long and is rated
PG-13.

Cautions: Some profanity and some childish "bathroom

humor." Preview the entire film for acceptability before using the program.

Materials:
 Jack video
 TV and VCR
 Construction paper or lightweight poster board
 Colored markers or pencils
 Yarn
 Clear, self-adhesive vinyl (contact paper)
 Paper punch.

Synopsis: Jack Powell has a unique condition that causes him to develop physically four times faster than normal. At the age of ten, he has the body of a forty-year-old. His parents homeschool him to shield him from the cruelty of other children until they are finally persuaded to let him go to school. Eventually, Jack fits in with the other kids until angina reminds his parents that Jack's time is limited. They pull him out of school. Miserable, he convinces them to let him return and face the risks inherent in life. On high school graduation day, now with the body of a 68-year-old, he delivers a commencement address advising everyone not to fear the future.

Icebreaker: Begin with a welcome and a prayer. An appropriate prayer would be: "Holy God, we are your sons and daughters. May we always come to you like children who recognize you as our loving parent. In Jesus' name we pray. Amen."
 If the young people do not all know each other, ask them to introduce themselves. As they do, have everyone name some qualities of children. Which of those are childlike? Which are childish? Which are also qualities of saints?

Discussion and learning: First, view the scene where Dr. Woodruff compares Jack and his extraordinary life to a shooting star that you see only once in a lifetime. Then view the scene where Jack's friend Louis tells his classmates what he wants to be when he grows up. Louis describes how Jack's childlike qualities make him "like the perfect grown-up." Finally, view Jack's commencement address.

If the group is more than six, divide into smaller discussion groups. At the end, have one person from each group report back to the larger group on their response to the following questions:

1. Is Jack really "like the perfect grown-up" as Louis says?
2. Have a volunteer in each group read aloud Luke 18:15-17. Is Jack a child in the way that Jesus means?
3. Have a volunteer read aloud Luke 12:22-31. How does this Scripture reflect Jack's views on worry and his ability to cope with life day to day? How is this passage similar to Mr. Woodruff's comparison of Jack and a shooting star?
4. When have any of you felt the peace that comes with living this way? What are ways that you can begin today that will enable you to enter God's kingdom as a child?

Learning activities: As a hands-on, "childish" learning activity, have the youth make bookmarks. As they work on this project, ask them to recall what it was like creating crafts like this in kindergarten, elementary school or Sunday school. Ask the youth how they view themselves now, how they remember their childish past, and how they foresee their future.

Let them cut card stock or construction paper into 2-by-6 strips. Have them write an appropriate Biblical quote—either one from this program or another that applies—on one side and the word "Jack" in large letters on the other. Cover in clear self-adhesive vinyl paper to laminate surfaces. Punch a hole near the top and add yarn, using a simple knot.

Closing: Point out that Jack is right when he says that life is fleeting. That is what makes it precious—too precious to waste with worry or fear. Ask the youths to complete this sentence: "I should stop worrying about—" Let any youth who wants to reveal his or her worry to the group do so. Verbalizing our worry helps us deal with it and allows others to help through reassurance and prayer.

As an additional learning activity beyond the video, have the youth investigate volunteer possibilities in homes, residential programs, camps, etc. for intellectually challenged adults. Have them give of their time visiting the residents or planning and carrying out a social activity such as birthday party for all, picnic or other outing.

SESSION TWO: *Hook*

I have set before you life and death, the blessing and the curse. Choose life, then, so that you and your descendants may live. (Deuteronomy 30:19b)

Theme: God calls us to make important choices in the adventure of life and to live according to their consequences.

Purpose: Youth will understand that part of growing up is making the choice to live—without fear.

Background: Hook (1992) is 144 minutes long and rated PG.

Cautions: Hook contains some vulgar language. Preview the entire film for acceptability before using the program.

Materials:
   Hook video
   TV and VCR
   Clear, self-adhesive vinyl paper
   Glitter and small stars

Two cardboard frames per person approximately 4-by-6
with an inside opening about 2 1/2-by-4 ½
Colored cellophane
Pieces of yarn about 5 inches long to be used as a hanger.

Synopsis: High-powered executive Peter Banning has little
time for his two children until they are kidnapped by a
man named James Hook. The crime and Peter's
swashbuckling effort to save his children lead him to the
astonishing revelation that Peter Banning is Peter Pan
grown up. Peter eventually recaptures his lost memory
and the ability to fly (with the help of some young
instructors) in time to defeat perennial foe Captain Hook.
Peter also comes to the final realization, in his last
spoken words of the movie, that "to live will be an
awfully great adventure."

Icebreaker: Begin with a welcome and a prayer. An
appropriate prayer would be: "Holy God, you are the
author of all life. May we seize each day gratefully as
your unique gift to us. In Jesus' name we pray. Amen."

If there are any new participants, ask them to
introduce themselves. As they do, have them discuss
whether they can recall ever not wanting to grow up, or
a time in their recent lives when they wished they were a
little kid again.

Discussion and learning: To introduce the scenes from *Hook*,
point out that fear of death made Peter want to not grow
up, because he knows that everyone who grows up has
to die. In the end, he conquers the fear of death by
choosing to live life as a great adventure.

First, show the scene where Peter sees himself as a
child. Watch how Peter's inner child—seen as his
reflection in water and as his shadow—calls him back to
the memory of who he is. Next, show the scene where
Peter, battling Hook, says that death will be a great
adventure. Finish with the last few minutes of the film.

Ask youth to listen for the words "death" and "live" in all of the video segments.

If the group is more than six, divide into smaller discussion groups. At the end, have one person from each group report back to the larger group on their response to the following questions:

1. What does Peter imply when he says "To live will be an awfully big adventure!"
2. What is the Biblical attitude toward life and death?
3. How do you think Jesus would react to the philosophy "Seize the day!"?
4. Sometimes we are called to put aside childish things and yet remain childlike, as represented by Peter's shadow self. Peter recognizes fatherhood is an adult responsibility. What are some other adult responsibilities?

Learning activities: For a "childish" activity, have the youth make suncatchers. To make a suncatcher, cut a piece of clear, self-adhesive vinyl about one inch larger than the opening in the cardboard frames. Peel off the paper backing to expose the sticky surface. Arrange glitter, stars, etc. on sticky side of the vinyl. Place a piece of pastel or clear cellophane against the sticky side of the plastic with the glitter sandwiched between. Glue one cardboard frame on each side of the sandwiched vinyl, with a yarn hanger attached between the layers. Trim away any excess vinyl.

Closing: Point out that making choices and accepting the consequences is part of maturity. Growing and living are choices. Ask the youth to complete this sentence: "My happy thought that helps me to live without fear is..."

As an additional learning activity, have the youth identify homebound seniors in their church or local community. They could visit them regularly or begin a pen-pal relationship.

Session Three: *Big*

When I was a child, I used to talk as a child, think as a child, reason as a child; when I became a man, I put aside childish things. (1 Corinthians 13:11)

Theme: God calls us to maturity.

Purpose: Youth will learn that the quest for maturity involves the painful process of leaving some aspects of childhood behind.

Background: *Big* (1988) is 104 minutes long and is rated PG.

Cautions: *Big* contains some profanity and implied sexual relations. Preview the entire film for acceptability before using the program.

Synopsis: Josh, a 13-year-old boy, makes a wish at a carnival to be big. In a textbook "be careful what you wish for" scenario, his wish is granted when he wakes up the next morning in a 30-year-old body. Although he becomes vice president of a toy company because of his instincts about what will sell to kids, he remains a kid at heart. He begins to "put aside childish things" only when he gets into a romantic relationship with a co-worker. But when he has a chance to go back to the carnival and return to childish things by reversing his wish, he does.

Materials:
    Big video
    TV and VCR
    Magazines, glue, scissors and "big" drawing paper.

Icebreaker: Begin with a welcome and an appropriate prayer, such as: "Holy God, you call us to grow in maturity and responsibility as we grow in our relationship with you. We ask your help in giving up whatever holds us back. In Jesus' name we pray. Amen."

    If there are any new participants, ask them to introduce themselves. As they do, have them name a

favorite toy from their childhood and tell when they
stopped playing with it, what they did with the toy, what
that felt like.

Discussion and learning: Point out that *Big* is the story of a
13-year-old who remains a boy despite acquiring a man's
body. Notice in the first segment all the ways he is
reminded that he's a kid. When he wakes up he is no
longer a kid physically—he has outgrown his clothes.
But the second segment shows that he is still a child
inside. Pay special attention to the last words of this
segment.

Show from the scene at the amusement park through
the point where Josh attempts to put on his clothes. Then
show the scene where Josh is playing with toys in his
office through when Susan says "He's a grown-up." Ask
the youth to discuss what they saw in the clips.

If the group is more than six participants, divide into
smaller discussion groups. At the end, have one person
from each group report back to the larger group on their
responses to these questions:

1. Why does Josh wish to be big?
2. How do we know that Josh is still a boy inside?
3. Why does Susan say that Josh is a grown-up?
4. Is she right? What do you think she is, or isn't?
5. How grown up is Paul, Josh's rival?
6. Jesus said, "You will never enter God's kingdom
   unless you enter it like a child" (Luke 18:17). Is
   Jesus contradicting Saint Paul in his letter to the
   Corinthians ?

Learning activities: Have the youth make a collage about
growing up. If there are enough youth in the group,
divide them into four groups. Assign each group a
different age level: infant/toddler/pre-schooler,
elementary school age, teenager, and adult. Have
participants collect pictures, words, and other images
from the magazines to illustrate each age. Hang

completed collages as "window panes" on the board or wall. Discuss the picture choices and tie the discussion to ages, appropriate activities, etc.

Closing: Point out that Josh ultimately realizes that he is not really grown up and that he opts to return to his parents. Ironically, this is a mature choice. He is going where he really belongs. Ask the youths to complete this sentence: "Something I realized during this session was . . ."

As an additional learning activity, have the youth group work with pre-school kids in Sunday school. If there is no Sunday school, they could create a two-hour activity with a group of pre-schoolers from church in which they play with them and teach them Bible stories. During this time they could reflect on what it means to put aside childish things and what it means for an adult to be like a child.

NINE

Ministry Online

Parishes are rushing into cyberspace with E-mail and their own Web sites. And well they should, for their members and prospective members are already online waiting for them. The question for faith communities shouldn't be whether to use the new technology, but how.

If your parish doesn't already have a place in cyberspace, you may be most worried about mechanical questions such as: How do we get space on a server? What will it cost? What software should we use to edit the site? Those are all great questions—to which I don't have the answers. I'm not a technical person, for starters, and there's no national one-size-fits-all solution anyway. Your diocese or archdiocese may be able to help. But the best approach, unless your diocese mandates use of a particular Web company (unlikely), is to find someone in your parish who creates or edits Web sites, either for a living or as a hobby. Most likely you'll find more than one, maybe through your youth club. (My daughter had designed three Web sites by the time she was eighteen.) A parish volunteer or a committee can create your site and help you find an Internet Service Provider, possibly one that provides free server space to non-profits.

Those technical issues may be the scariest part of starting a Web site, but they aren't the most important. The mechanics of the site are necessary, but not sufficient. You can't use the site well, or even know how to use it, until you're clear about what you want its mission to be. That's no small decision.

Types of Religious Web Sites

When Cardinal Roger Mahoney of Los Angeles called cyberspace "a new Sea of Galilee along which Jesus and others can walk," he seemed to be thinking of the Internet as a medium for evangelization, or at least pre-evangelization. But that's only one purpose for which religious Web sites are used. I've identified seven kinds of sites. You may distinguish others as you surf the Net looking at religious Web sites to get ideas for your own. This category business is inexact anyway, a blunt tool to help you think about what a parish Web site *can* do and what yours *should* do. Few sites fit totally into one category with no elements of any other. But most are predominantly one of the following:

Informational. Information is an inescapable element of any Web page. But in some, information is the overriding component. For example, The Presbyterian Church U.S.A. Web site (www.pcusa.org) announces itself at the top as "Starting point for information about the Presbyterian Church (U.S.A.)" The welcome page of the official Web site of the United Methodist Church (www.umc.org) is packed with buttons to call up informational pages—about the church, about church finances, about church leadership. Appropriately, an earlier version of the site was called "United Methodist Information."

Informational Web sites may exist for any number of reasons (to educate, to promote, or to advertise, for example) and different types of audience (members, potential members, community at large, customers for products). Your site probably needs to have a strong informational content to satisfy those looking for it. But Web pages also offer the opportunity to give visitors what they aren't looking for—an invitation to a stronger relationship with their Lord. More on that later.

Whatever the purpose and audience, the sites I categorize as informational also tend to be highly institutional. They're full of information about the church as a physical reality in a certain dimension (parish, diocese, synod). But they have little to say about the church as a metaphysical reality, the Body of Christ. They don't give the kind of information embodied in catechesis or doctrine, and have little power to "make disciples of all nations" (Matthew 28:20).

Apologetic. One apologetic Web site, Catholic Answers (www.catholic.com), defines apologetics in the course of its self-description: "Since we are Catholic apologists, we defend and explain the Catholic faith, helping people to understand its teachings better, including the basis for them in Scripture, the Early Church Fathers, and the documents of the Church. We also defend Catholic beliefs and practices from attacks made by anti-Catholics of various persuasions."

Apologetics doesn't just inform; it argues. As the names of "Catholic Answers" and the equally apologetic "Christian Answer Network" (www.christiananswers.net) from the Evangelical Christian perspective imply, apologetic sites carry the presumption that there are always logical answers to questions of faith. Apologetics speaks to the mind from the perspective of Enlightenment rationality, while evangelism—sharing the Good News—appeals to the whole person.

Clearinghouse. These sites are gateways to a whole host of other sites with a common religious orientation. Gospel Communication Network (www.gospelcom.net), for example, is an evangelical megasite, an alliance of 163 Christian ministries. Catholic clearinghouses include Catholic Goldmine (www.catholicgoldmine.com), Catholic Information Network on the Internet (www.catholic.net), Catholic Educators Resources (www.silk.net/RelEd) and Catholic Online (www.catholic.org). There seem to be new ones every month.

Chaplaincy. A parish site could be so oriented toward taking care of its own with parish and school information that it has virtually nothing to offer a visitor who isn't a member—it's totally "in-house." It may be, in effect, the parish bulletin online, with no links that establish it as part of a broader church community. This isn't outreach, which the Internet is ideally suited for, but a kind of virtual pastoral care.

Spiritual. Spirituality, like information and chaplaincy, is a component of many sites and the driving force of some. It's hardly surprising that the Web sites of the Taizé Community (www.taize.fr) and the Monastery of Christ in the Desert (www.christdesert.org) are spiritual sites, and wonderful ones. But a parish site could incorporate a heavy dose of spirituality as well. I once saw one that did, although when I checked back a few years later it had been transformed into an almost totally informational site.

Marketing. Marketing sites exist to "sell" something, usually a parish, by promising to meet the visitor's needs. What the church believes often seems to be not as important as what it's selling—good fellowship, rousing services, and a host of ministries to take care of members.

The Ginghamsburg Church (www.ginghamsburg.org) , a fast-growing megachurch that uses electronic media heavily in its services, answers the classic marketing question "What's in it for me?" with such statements as: "Ginghamsburg Church has been a great place for my wife, Carolyn, and me to raise our family. A relevant and contemporary setting for worship, upbeat music, education, recreation and fellowship is offered for both followers of Christ and those contemplating the Christian life." This feels less like drawing a soul to Christ than pitching a potential customer.

Christian Answers Network, though primarily apologetic, shows a similar disposition. It has a button that poses the question "Is Jesus Christ the Answer to Your Questions?" It answers by saying: "Yes, Jesus Christ can help you find the answers you have been searching for. He can supply your needs and give comfort to those who hurt. He will give you rest in this weary world and bring understanding to your mind. All Jesus asks is that you receive Him as your savior and friend." Like most televangelists, the site is long on happiness and short on suffering.

The problem with any church marketing, including marketing-oriented Web sites, is the temptation to alter the church's message to grab market share. But some sites demonstrate that it's possible to use cyberspace to proclaim the Gospel of Jesus without twisting it into a consumerist panacea. This is especially true of evangelistic sites.

Evangelistic. Christian evangelism is sharing the Good News, rather than facts; it's an invitation into the life of Christ, not a promise to meet identified needs; it's reaching beyond the choir, sent by Jesus (John 20:21) to make disciples of all nations (Matthew 20:28). By identifying some Web sites as evangelistic, I'm not saying that they evangelize in the truest sense of the term. They're actually pre-evangelization, preparation for the gospel. Evangelization demands one-on-one witness—an embodied believer. But evangelistic Web sites share, invite and reach out to people who have walked by your church without going in. They do so in a remarkably broad range of ways.

The Diocese of Greensburg, Pennsylvania (www. catholicgbg.org), makes its invitation into the life of Christ more explicit than any other I have seen. After posing a few questions like, "What does it mean to be a Christian today?" and "Can prayer make a difference in my life?" it says: "The people of the Catholic Diocese of Greensburg invite you to join us as we explore these and many other challenging questions encountered on life's journey. Come along, as we journey with Jesus Christ, on the faith Journey of a Lifetime."

The Byzantine Catholic Eparchy of Passaic site (http://member.aol.com/byzruth) is informational in what it says with words. But its icons, lavishly used throughout the site, perhaps evangelize more than words could. If the down side of the image culture is "image" in the shallow sense replacing reality, the up side is the power of images to form and transform. This site exemplifies that.

Some sites tell stories with evangelizing power. The *St. Anthony Messenger* site (www.AmericanCatholic.org) has a Saint of the Day hagiography feature. The Monastery of Christ in the Desert presents "Stories from the Desert Fathers," which the site describes as "Wisdom from the earliest Christian monks, preserved by their disciples and handed on to their descendants." The Desert Fathers material, like the stories of saints, isn't propositional. These stories function like myths or parables in that they tell truths in ways that transcend doctrine or easy explanation. They say a lot in a few words, usually telling of the actions of some famous monk.

St. Paul Catholic Church in Englewood, Ohio (www.siscom.net/~epistle), devotes a major section of its site to "St. Paul's Faith Formation Process." Under the heading of "General Introduction and Philosophy," the faith formation section talks eloquently about the centrality of Mass, the sacraments, and the Scriptures as the "School of Faith" for Catholic Christians. "If these are not the center of every Catholic's life, nothing else makes any sense," the site notes. The "Liturgical Calendar" section is much more than a calendar. It's also a powerful explanation of how the journey of faith proceeds through time marked by feasts and seasons closely tied to the life of Christ: "By entering into the cycle of feasts and seasons we enter more deeply into the mystery of Christ who is all times and seasons, the beginning and the end of our lives. This is, after all, the purpose of religious education: being in Christ."

Do you want your Web site to inform, to argue for the faith, to point the way to other Web sites, to give pastoral care to your own parishioners, to offer spiritual sustenance, to market, or to evangelize? That's probably not the question. The question is: In what proportion do you want to do each of those things? To what do you want to devote the most content and the most prominent position on your welcome page?

My own belief, as the Webmaster for the Archdiocese of Cincinnati's Web site (www.CatholicCincinnati.org), is that evangelization is the church's highest and best use of the Internet. It's the use that most fully carries the mission of the church into cyberspace and maximizes the Net's ability to reach out in a way that a parish bulletin or diocesan newspaper usually doesn't. Our Web site began as a cyberspace version of the local Catholic directory. The welcome page was mostly words, with a few photos—a highly informational site. It was a great place to start, but I changed the look and added content.

Today an image of a Celtic Cross dominates the welcome page. At the very heart of the cross are the words "What does it mean to be Catholic?" That links to an original article by the assistant director of the religious education office in charge of evangelization. Other points of the cross address the questions "How Can I Return to the Church?" (about our "Come Home" program), "What Does the Church Teach?" (linking to *The Catechism of the Catholic Church*), and "How Can I Become Catholic?" (about RCIA). "Keeping the Lord's Day" links to Cincinnati Archbishop Daniel E. Pilarczyk's five-part series of articles on Sunday worship and Sunday rest.

Other buttons on the page take visitors to the readings of the day (at www.nccbuscc.org), the Saint of the Day (www.AmericanCatholic.org), and Sunday readings and homily (an audio link to the homily from our TV mass). The visitor also can click into *The Catholic Telegraph*, our archdiocesan newspaper which is heavily oriented toward adult faith formation, and *Live Letters*, Archbishop Pilarczyk's weekly series about the second readings on Sunday. This material that I consider evangelistic takes center stage on the welcome page. Buttons accessing factual material about the bishops and the offices of the Archdiocese go down the left. Links, news releases, a calendar, and more go down the right.

What should *your* parish Web site look like? What should it contain? That depends on what you want it to accomplish. But whether you want your site to be evangelistic or informational, it's important that it be done well. Better designed Web sites do gain bigger audiences. The church faces stiff competition in cyberspace, just as she does everywhere else. Here are a few observations about creating successful Web sites:

Design

The central image and words on the welcome page are crucial because they tell visitors right off what the designers and
sponsors of the site must think is most important. At the Web
site of St. Francis of Assisi Catholic Church in Centerville,
Ohio (www.bright.net/~sfa), for example, the dominant
image on the welcome page is a quilt made out of squares
representing each family of the parish, with a cross at the center of the quilt. The message couldn't be clearer: The cross of
Jesus Christ is at the heart of this parish, and its Web site
delivers that Good News. It's primarily an evangelistic site,
with buttons on the welcome page to find out more about
"Mission" and "Beliefs." Try to come up with a central image
for your welcome page that's a metaphor of what you're
about. Put the less important but still necessary material on
the sides.

Web sites should do what the Web can do well—illustrate.
But be careful not to burden your pages with too many illus-
trations; they take a long time to download and surfers won't
wait. Web pages can also make good use of sound, although
few religious Web sites have taken advantage of that.

Content

No matter how spiritual or evangelistic you want your Web
site to be, it has to contain a certain amount of informational
content: Names of key church leaders (ordained and lay),
Mass times, upcoming activities, anything that would go in
the parish bulletin. In fact, you can put the whole bulletin on
your site (while retaining the print version). What else? Ask
the folks who answer the phones at the parish. Whatever your
parish gets a lot of calls about should be addressed on its Web
site. RCIA is probably one such subject. Your Web site should
tell how RCIA works at this parish, when pre-catechumenate
meetings are held, whom to contact, and a form enabling Web
visitors to e-mail back their names and phone numbers if they
would prefer to *be* contacted. But don't stop there. Either cre-

ate or link to an explanation of what RCIA is all about and what the Catholic Church is all about. Give an informational piece an evangelistic dimension.

Bolster that evangelistic dimension by making the language accessible to everyone. Don't just have a button that says "RCIA." Most potential inquirers won't know what that means. Nor will they understand the term "pre-catechumenate," just as most "inactive Catholics" won't know that phrase means them. You might, instead, say something inviting like "I've thought about becoming Catholic" or "Maybe it's time for me to return to the church." That's a lot of words, but it takes a lot of words to be clear about this. You can make it up with briefer button labels like "Parish staff" and "Mass times."

The school is an important part of your parish and should occupy a good chunk of your Web site. In addition to providing a range of information from how to enroll to important dates on the school calendar, put some of the students' work on the Web site. That will be a learning experience for them and for their parents, who will be lured into the site by their children. (But don't put photos of school children on the Web where anyone can see them; that understandably makes parents nervous.)

An unavoidable feature of the cyberculture is fascination with the new. "What's New" segments, especially when in motion, build traffic on Web pages. One of the great things about Web sites is that they *can* be updated frequently. One of the bad things is that they *must* be updated frequently. A really timely message at the wrong time sends a bad message, as did the parish that greeted me with an Advent message on March 16. (That parish had the right concept, though, in trying to reflect the liturgical calendar on the welcome page. It's more important than your parish and school calendar of activities.) Designate a staff member or responsible parish volunteer to keep the content of the Web site fresh. That keeps visitors coming back. If you can't make it look new, at least don't make it look old. Avoid timely messages altogether unless you're sure you can replace them when they're no longer current.

Use lots of links. Visitors expect to find them. More importantly, linking to the Vatican (www.vatican.va), to the National Conference of Catholic Bishops/United States Catholic Conference (www.nccbuscc,org), to your (arch)diocese and others around the country, and to Catholic organizations in your area makes a statement that your parish doesn't stand alone but is part of the church universal. Check out some of the Catholic clearinghouse sites to find sites you might want to link to. Whenever you want to link, the etiquette of the Internet is to e-mail the Webmaster of the other site and ask permission first. Also ask for a link to your site.

Strive for interactivity on your Web pages, even though you probably can't do live chat as a parish Web site. Include E-mail addresses of parish staff members and members of the parish pastoral council, parish commissions and other parish organizations. Other interactive features might include:

An opportunity to post prayer requests.

A "visitors book" where non-parishioners who have visited can post their impressions of the community.

Support materials for the school and the parish school of religion, including interactive homework. (You could also provide E-mail links to teachers. But some teachers tell me they prefer to talk with parents in person or on the phone. The interaction is immediate and teachers can pick up helpful non-verbal cues from the parents.)

A bulletin board open for comment on the Sunday homily, not just as feedback to the preacher but to open dialogue in the parish that keeps the homily and the Sunday readings alive through the week. (Your priests and deacons have to be really brave for this one.)

In addition to being as interactive as possible in cyberspace, all content areas on the site should also offer the opportunity to be interactive in person (or by telephone). List an updated name and phone number of the contact person for each subject area (RCIA for inquirers, Remembering Church for inactive Catholics, etc.) Parish staffers should follow up on cyber contacts with personal contact when appropriate. Above all, it is absolutely essential that no one asking to be contacted is ignored. Someone needs to check and route E-mail inquiries no less than daily.

Cyberspace does many wonderful things, but it can't replace a local church community. The church can't exist in cyberspace any more than it can exist on television, although both can be ways of inviting people into the church. A parish Web site should always invite a physical visit—real presence—as many do.

Just as many parishes have added ramps or elevators to increase access to their church, you ought to make sure that your place in cyberspace is accessible. Elderly and shut-ins in a parish could benefit greatly from electronic connection to their parish, to others online, and to the whole world through the Web. Computers aren't just for kids—senior citizens often show a remarkable eagerness and ability to "surf the Net." But many don't have the knowledge to use a computer or the money to buy one. Why not launch a parish project to equip such folks with used modem-equipped computers donated by other parishioners who are upgrading? And for their mentors, the parish could match homebound parishioners with computer-savvy youngsters, perhaps confirmation candidates or high school students in community service. Older and younger parishioners would forge a human connection as well as a computer connection. The parish could pick up the cost for a basic Internet connection service.

You're never going to get everyone in the parish connected, though, so make sure that everything you have in cyberspace is available at the parish center in hard copy or reprinted frequently in the bulletin. You don't want to leave anyone out.

Getting the Word Out

If it's important to have a Web site, it's important to let people *know* you have a Web site, both within the parish and outside of it. Here's a basic publicity plan for your site:

Make announcements about it at Mass.

Run repeated stories about it in the parish bulletin and any other parish publications. Don't wait until the site is finished (it never is anyway) but build ownership by soliciting ideas for content as you go along.

Put up posters around the parish.

Print your Web address on your bulletin each week and on your business cards, ads, stationery, and newsletters that go home with school children.

Make a series of presentations on the Web site to parish organizations; tell them what they can get out of the site and what they can put into it.

Get the school involved: If some of the classes go online, make sure they visit your (their) parish Web site. Have teachers urge students to take their parents to the site.

Send a press release to your (arch)diocesan newspaper about the site for external publicity. Also link to the diocesan Web site and ask the Webmaster to link to your site.

Register with search engines so that Web surfers will be able to find you. You can do that at www.submitit.com and www.webposition.com.

For Reflection

- *Is there a danger that the attractive design or "bells and whistles" (music, animation) of your Web site will capture more attention than its message? Why or why not?*

- *Can the church ever offer sacraments online? Why or why not?*

- *Some dioceses have put a Sunday mass on their Web site. Do you think this is a good idea? Why or why not?*

TEN

Meet the Press

Until now we haven't considered the aspect of the media age which may be the most challenging for pastors and other pastoral ministers, especially in times of crisis—the news media.

It may not happen a lot, but at times in your ministry you'll want to get something from the news media (favorable coverage of an event or milestone). At other times, they'll want something from you (comment or information, possibly on a matter of controversy). In the first situation, you're the initiator, you're proactive. In the second, you're forced to be reactive. Since that's a more demanding role, let's start there. Consider three familiar scenarios:

You've fired a popular catechist who insisted on fudging the church's teachings on divorce, homosexuality and ordination. The liberals are upset.

You've renovated the sanctuary, moving the tabernacle to a separate Blessed Sacrament chapel. The conservatives are upset.

You've discontinued Thursday night bingo, ending a forty-year parish tradition. The gamblers are *really* upset.

Cases like these, and many others that you could think of, cause dissension and controversy in a parish. Sometimes disgruntled parishioners can manage to get a newspaper or a TV station to report on the discontent. That's bad public relations, bad for the church as a whole. How does a pastoral staff avoid that, keeping a controversial situation in the parish from becoming a contentious one in the news? The time to worry about that is long before the news media have a chance to get interested.

Seven Habits of Effective Parish Communications

By the time a reporter shows up at the door of the parish center, you've already missed your best chances to soothe hurt feelings and maintain Christian community in the face of disagreements over policy. You have to start with good internal communications. Developing seven habits of highly effective parish communications, while not magic, will go a long way toward creating good PR inside and outside the parish. Then you needn't dread a reporter's phone call or appearance on the scene.

HABIT #1. *First, Do the Right Thing.* It's relatively easy to communicate and defend a controversial action or policy when it's right. It's much harder to communicate with conviction a move that's unjust, confusing or inconsistent. So be sure that you have solid reasons for what you're doing and can articulate them to parishioners, school parents or the press. The best public relations is good policy, equitably enforced.

HABIT #2. *Be the First With the News.* Try to make sure you're the first to get out the word about an action that's likely to be controversial. That means you should go public as soon as a decision is final. Otherwise parishioners may hear an inaccurate version through the rumor mill, a slanted version from opponents, or a sensationalized version through the news media. Communicating with your people before the rumors start or the news stories appear will gain you trust and loyalty.

HABIT #3. *Don't Squash Controversy—Confront It.* Seize the teaching moment by meeting arguments head-on. Allow opponents to air different points of view. The most divisive situations are those in which people feel that they haven't been heard, informed, or considered. Let everyone know you've heard them, even if you don't agree with them.

HABIT #4. *The Best Rumor Control Technique Is the Truth— Told Quickly and Fully.* Sometimes you have to give out information you'd rather not. That should be done as soon as possible—to the stakeholders first, then to the broader community if appropriate. And when the truth hurts, tell it anyway. The Pontifical Council for Social Communications, in the 2000 document "Ethics in Communications," says bluntly: "Those who represent the church must be honest and straightforward in their relations with journalists." Start by being honest and straightforward with your own people.

HABIT #5. *Be Prepared to React.* Sometimes the news gets out and the angry or troubled calls start coming before you have a chance to announce it, or even catch your breath. You have to be ready for that as soon as you've taken any action— or someone has taken an action against you!—that will cause concern in the parish. If you're the point person, marshal your facts and your arguments before you deal with the issue. Begin your response to parishioners with a sincere statement of understanding and sympathy about their concern.

HABIT #6. *Don't Dodge the News Media.* When a situation has parish stakeholders upset, confused or worried, the news media may take an interest. If your diocesan communications policy permits it, parish officials should agree to interview requests and should be as forthcoming as possible while respecting the privacy rights of everyone involved. If you don't tell your side of the story, no one will. The story will be written or broadcast anyway, perhaps with speculation you could have refuted or errors you could have corrected. And a "no comment" from the parish makes it look like the church is hiding something. Be civil and cooperative, even if the reporter is not. An argument with a reporter is an argument you can't win. The journalist always gets the last word. But most reporters don't have axes to grind—they have deadlines to meet and editors to satisfy. Their mistakes are usually due to ignorance, not malice. So each contact with a reporter is also a teaching moment. Being cooperative doesn't mean you have to act against your own interest, though. If you're approached for an interview and the thought makes you physically ill, either get another well informed person to speak for the parish or present your side of the story in a written statement. And if a TV crew shows up shooting video of your school kids, politely ask them to leave your property because you don't want to put those students at risk. (But you can't prevent them shooting from across the street.)

HABIT #7. *Public Relations Is Everybody's Concern, Not Just the Pastor's.* While you don't want a parish volunteer talking to reporters in the name of the parish, everyone connected with the parish represents the parish to the rest of the world to some degree—especially staffers. Anyone who works for the parish should receive at least minimal training in dealing with people, particularly angry people. Every phone call should be returned and every caller, no matter how off the wall, should be treated courteously.

The Care and Feeding of Reporters

Dealing with reporters can be scary if you aren't used to it—and scarier if you are. So let's look a little closer at how to do that.

When a reporter calls, first be clear you know what station or newspaper the reporter is calling from and what the reporter covers. If it's the police reporter, you should be a little more concerned and wary than if it's the religion reporter or a feature writer.

Make sure you get the reporter's name and phone number so you can call back if necessary.

If your secretary or your voice mail took the call while you were away, call the reporter back as soon as possible. If you don't, the reporter may look for another church to get a nice photo of an Ash Wednesday service, for example. When the reporter is calling about something controversial at your parish, that's even more reason to call back quickly. Do so even if you can't say much about the issue. The reporter deserves to know where he or she stands.

Some reasons why you may not be able to discuss the matter in any substance include: 1) Diocesan policy says you can't. In this case, refer the reporter to the diocesan communications officer. 2) Legalities. "We haven't seen the lawsuit yet, so we can't comment on it." "That matter is in litigation, so unfortunately we can't say anything about it right now." "The employee hasn't been charged, so it would be inappropriate to give a name." 3) You haven't told the people who should hear it from you, not the evening news. "Yes, we've made a decision on the future of the school and that's what our parish meeting tonight is about. That's when we'll talk about it." The flip side of this is that you should be willing to say for the media anything you've already said in a public document or is public knowledge. And if more than a handful of people have received a letter, it's a public document. Somebody will fax a copy to the reporter anyway, so you might as well be cooperative. 4) You simply don't know enough. "We don't have all the facts yet and we don't want to speculate."

Don't get drawn into an interview over the phone before you even know it. Unless you've already been through this issue so many times that you know exactly what to say and how to say it, it's a good idea to ask to call the reporter right back. Then take a few minutes to collect your thoughts and any supportive data that might help. Fax the reporter any printed material that might help, such as a fact sheet.

When you agree to an interview, you have every right to set ground rules if you wish. Tell the reporter what you will talk about and what you won't talk about, how long you can talk, what you will allow to be taped for TV. "I can tell you what we're missing and what we're doing to beef up security, but I can't say anything about the former employee. That's a police matter."

In any interview with a reporter, even if it's just a few minutes on the telephone, you have an agenda just as the reporter does. You want to get across your own message, not just answer the reporter's questions. So your most important task is to keep the interview message-driven, not question-driven. Determine your objective—what you want to accomplish with this interview—and no more than three message points to further that objective. Develop these points into sound bites that you can work into your answers. You need to be brief, simple, accurate, jargon-free, cliche-free, natural and strong.

For example: An eighth grade student who threatened to shoot another student has been suspended from school. The suspended student didn't actually have a gun. You realize that some people will think this action is too strong and others will think it's too weak. As the pastor or principal, you decide that your main goal in this interview is to make it clear that your school is a safe place for parents to send their children— because you work to keep it that way. How do you establish that? *By noting that:* 1) "No students were ever actually in any danger." 2) "To maintain a safe learning environment for the protection of all our children, we have a zero tolerance policy on threats." 3) "We care about the student who was suspended and we want him to get some help before we let him come back to school." And you start out with a sincere message of concern: "This situation has many parents upset, and rightly so. We take this very seriously. But it's important to remember that no students were ever actually in any danger."

All of these same points should already be in a letter sent home with the students as soon as the disciplinary action was taken. (*Habit #2: Be first with the news.*) Stick closely to that script. When a question takes the interview off your message point, pull it back. "Yes, it's true that one of the younger children overheard the threat and screamed. But at no point was that first-grader or any other student in any danger. There was no weapon involved." Don't worry about being repetitious. Stating your key points several times increases your chances of hitting just the right combination of words that strikes the reporter as the perfect sound bite to summarize what you're trying to say.

Dos and Don'ts of Media Interviews:

Don't:

Say merely "no comment" or "I don't know." That sounds like you're hiding something, are uninformed, or are being uncooperative. Give reasons why you can't answer a question at this time or say you don't know but will find out.

Say anything inappropriate for an official of the church, such as foul or spiteful language.

Lie or exaggerate. Remember "Ethics in Communications" and be "honest and straightforward" with reporters, even when that entails admitting lapses or mistakes.

Guess the answer to a question. Instead, offer to find the information or refer the reporter elsewhere.

Speculate. Just refuse to answer hypothetical questions or questions of opinion.

Answer a question that hasn't been asked, except to deliver one of your message points that you've worked out in advance. For example, when you're asked how long the popular catechist was with the parish before you removed her, you can say, "Twenty years." Don't add: "She did a great job and people know her all over the country. She's written four books." However, it's okay to

add: "But she wasn't teaching what the church teaches.
Catechumens have a right to hear the official teachings of
the church, not just the catechist's opinion."

Rush to fill the silence if the reporter is mum after you've
answered a question. That's when you're most likely to
say something you shouldn't, which is why the long
pause is one of journalism's most effective techniques.

Argue with the reporter, lose your cool, be combative, or
hang up (as one priest did, which was duly reported in
the newspaper).

Say anything you don't want to see printed or broadcast.
Especially be careful not to say anything to a TV reporter
after the camera lights go off that you wouldn't say with
them on.

Let yourself be put on the defensive. Avoid repeating false
accusations ("anti-gay") or loaded phrases ("pro-choice")
in your answer. Instead, correct a false premise with a
positive statement at the beginning of your answer:
"First of all, the tabernacle is highly visible in the new
chapel. That location is highly suitable and easily
available for Eucharistic adoration." (You have
challenged the terminology "shoving the Blessed
Sacrament off into a corner" without repeating it.)

Do:

Repeat the question in the answer (as long as it doesn't
contain a false premise.) This makes it easier for the
reporter to use your quote in toto without having to set
it up. It also establishes beyond confusion what question
you're answering. Put another way, it makes clear what
you understand the question to be.

Tell the truth. Beyond not lying, make sure you have all the
facts straight.

Be helpful. Try to get the reporter the story he/she wants if
that story is accurate.

Control the interview. Remember to answer the reporter's
   question, but then segue into the points you have
   determined in advance to make. "But what's important
   here is . . ." "Let's not forget that . . ."

Be sure you understand the question and that the reporter
   understands the answer. It's okay to ask, "Is that clear?"
   "Do you see what I mean?" Don't worry about being too
   basic in explaining church terms. That's impossible.
   Correct any mistakes or misunderstandings immediately
   but politely.

Try to be both brief and quotable. Use those sound bites
   you've thought out in advance. If you keep the answer
   short, there's less chance of misstatement and more
   chance that your whole statement can be used and not
   cut in a way that's misleading. If you run on too long,
   the reporter has to edit it down based on his or her own
   judgement. It's better for you to edit yourself because
   then you get to decide what's most important instead of
   the reporter.

Be careful about using humor; it can be misunderstood.

Use examples, comparisons, statistics and people stories,
   including printed background material, to bolster your
   answers to follow-up questions.

Be as positive as possible in every answer. Doing all this with
   a newspaper reporter or even a radio reporter over the
   phone isn't so daunting for most people. But when a TV
   reporter says she'd like to do an on-camera interview,
   your sweat glands may get a workout. I've helped
   prepare a dozen or more people for their first TV
   interview, mostly school principals, and they all did well
   with no more experience than you've had. Remember
   three important points about TV interviews:

Dress appropriately. Sometimes casual is okay or even
   desirable. But if you want to speak from a position of
   authority, wear dress clothes. If you're a priest, wear the
   collar.

Work on eliminating the "uhs" that you're tempted to stick between words. They're annoying. Speaking slowly and deliberately will help cut this down.

Assemble in advance any charts, graphs, maps, paintings or video that may help you make your point.

When you've finished the interview, it's out of your hands. You can call back to add information, but forget about trying to see a copy of the story—even a newspaper story—in advance. Reporters don't have the time or the inclination to submit a story for your approval.

If the story turns out well you should affirm that by dropping the reporter a note. Commend the reporter's accuracy, not the fact that it was positive or helpful. You don't want the reporter to feel like your press agent or shill.

If there was a problem with the story, be sure you can articulate what it is. If the story is totally accurate but makes you or someone in your parish look bad because you bungled, it's hard to complain without looking like you're just protecting your self-interest. If the story misquotes you or lacks balance even though you presented your side of the story, then you have a legitimate beef and a range of options for responding.

The first option is to do nothing. Sometimes demanding a correction has the unwanted effect of extending the natural life of a negative story that would die if you keep quiet.

But other times you need to so something. Start with a phone call or letter to the reporter. When I was a newspaper reporter, I always resented it if a complainer went to my editor first. And when I was an editor, I always paid more attention when I knew that someone with an axe to grind had ground it on the reporter first. If you don't get what you ask for, then work your way up the journalistic food chain.

What you ask for can depend, too. One step up from doing nothing is simply asking that a corrective note be put in the news organization's library so that the mistake doesn't get made again. This is the course you can take when you don't want to resurrect a dead issue, but you don't want an old mistake to be repeated if the story comes to life again on its own.

When the issue is still alive anyway, or the mistake has so much potential for harm that it's worth keeping the story on life support for another day, you'll want to ask for a correction on the air or in print.

But here, too, there's an alternative if you're dealing with a newspaper. Writing a letter to the editor might be a better strategy than seeking a correction. This works especially well when you want to challenge the slant of a story, including loaded words and lack of balance. And even if your complaint is a major factual error, a letter to the editor might be preferable to a small correction on page two. A letter gives you some space to make an argument in one of the best read sections of the newspaper.

When You Want Coverage

One of the reasons to be as responsive as possible with news organizations is that someday you may need them as much as they need you now. When you want to get out the word to the general community—beyond your parish—about an event, an activity, a volunteer opportunity, a position on a local issue or any number of other things, you need your local newspapers (daily and weekly), radio stations and television stations to be your megaphone.

The only way you can totally control the message you send out is by buying advertising space in print or time on the air. That's not hard. All you need is money. If you don't have money, or much of it, you can try to get the news media to run news stories. That's a little trickier, but easier than you may think. After all, news organizations are in the business of reporting the news. All you have to do is convince them that what you have is news.

What is news? Surveying five college journalism textbooks, I couldn't find a definition of news. I found many listings of characteristics that make something newsworthy, but no definition of news. So I developed my own when I started teaching about news. As a former working journalist, I define news as:

1. a report (it's not news until it's reported)
2. of a previously unreported (not necessarily new, but unreported)
3. situation or occurrence (trends, as well as events, can be news)
4. of some significance or interest (somebody has to care)
5. to the target audience (page one in Paris, France may be page 48 in Paris, Kentucky).

Pay special attention to the fourth point—that's where news judgment comes in. Events are objective (concrete, factual), but news is a choice. A news report, like all media, is a constructed reality. It's always a view of the truth as the reporters and editors perceive it even though they're doing their best to be objective or—more realistically—fair.

Let's take a look at how journalists construct reality. Any news account is the end result of a long series of judgments. At least one reporter and at least one editor, but often more, have to decide:

what to cover (and not cover)
what to put in a story
what to leave out of a story
who to interview (and of that interview what to quote, what to paraphrase, what to leave out)
where to put the story on the newscast or in the newspaper (front page or features; first two minutes or last two minutes)
where to put the story on the page or within the segment
how much space or time to give it

These are all questions that you would have to deal with if you were reporter or editor for a day. And you'd have to do it quickly because you're facing deadlines every day, even on a weekly. So how do you get a story about your parish's new soup kitchen or its support group for post-abortive women on to the list of what to cover?

You have to convince a reporter (and, ultimately, an editor) that it's news—previously unreported and of interest to the newspaper or station's audience. What makes a potential story interesting? By the standards of traditional news judgment, readers and viewers should be able to identify with the story. They may do that because it affects them or because it deals with someone they know or know about, or because it packs an emotional punch—it's affective, in terms of those characteristics of the media age listed in chapter two. But today a story almost has to have at least some of the other characteristics as well: visual (a plus even for print), aural (especially for radio), commercial, entertaining, stimulating (big numbers or a surprising turn of events), simplistic (heavy theology usually won't make it), and/or immediate (happening now). If reporters and editors perceive your story as having one or more of those elements, it has a good chance to make it into "the news."

But you don't have just a story, you have a message. What do you want to say? To whom do you want to say it? Answers to those questions will help determine which media to approach. Not every message is suitable for every medium. If it's a parish-only event, maybe you don't need to go beyond your parish bulletin and Web site. But if you're trying to reach a larger audience, you'll have to aim higher—at TV, radio and newspapers (dailies, neighborhood weeklies, diocesan weekly).

I once heard a veteran religion reporter say, "Get to know us before you want to use us." He was talking about building long-term relationships with journalists, which is certainly important. Meet the religion reporters and any others you might have dealings with. But you should also get to know your local media in the sense of how each news organization approaches stories and what its regular features are. Getting to know the differences among local media may help you place a story. For example: If a local TV station or newspaper regularly carries a "Hometown Hero" feature about volunteers, that's the place to go with a story about your parish honoring the couple who have cared for the flowers in front of the church for twenty years.

If you're offering a feature story that seems to fit a niche at a particular news organization, the best way to pitch it may be a phone call supported by a fact sheet. If you have a story of more general interest, such as a parish retreat or a media literacy talk open to anyone, then send out a news release to all the local media. (In fact, if it's a really big story, other news outlets will get mad at you for giving an exclusive to a competitor and not notifying them.)

But don't stop there. If it's a highly visual event, press harder at TV stations with follow-up calls. If it's a story that takes some explanation, spend some time trying to interest the newspapers; they have the space to get into the more arcane aspects of religion coverage. And sometimes you can do both. A story about a parish pilgrimage involving twelve busloads of parishioners has a strong visual element to stress with TV stations and a strong theological underpinning to push with newspapers.

Type your press release, double spaced, on one side of an 8½-inch by 11-inch paper. Use letterhead stationery, with your parish logo, on the front page. Keep it simple and keep it short—preferably one page, and certainly no more than two. (I have even cheated on spacing, making it slightly less than double spaced to make the release fit on one page.) Structure the news release in what is called "inverted pyramid" style, meaning that you put the most important news or the most attention-getting aspect first. If your parish is going to baptize an entire family of thirteen people at the Easter vigil, put that in the first sentence of the release about the vigil, not buried near the end. Be sure your release answers all of the traditional journalistic questions of who, what, when, where, why and how. And because you still won't cover everything, include a contact name, phone number and E-mail address that reporters can use for further information. Make sure the contact is someone who can actually be contacted, not someone who is seldom available.

Most press releases these days are faxed or e-mailed,

which saves on both time and postage. Using WinFax or similar software, you can fax directly from your computer to a stored database of media fax numbers. If the release is about an event open to the public, do this about ten days before the event. That's enough time for the media to run stories in advance, yet not so far in advance that it's likely to get lost in the shuffle. If you want coverage as well as advance notice, call with a reminder a couple of days before the event. Most of the time you do want coverage, even for a one-day event. It builds awareness and interest for next time.

If you have a story so hot you know reporters will be besieging you for comment—the pope having lunch in your rectory, for example—the way to make that manageable is to hold a news conference. That gets all the media together at one time and place with an equal shot at the same sound bites. It's unlikely you'll ever need to do this. If you do, send out a release to announce the news conference just a couple of hours before starting time. Otherwise, reporters will hound you so they can get the story before competing media. The announcement has to tell enough to get reporters there but not the whole story. For example, you could send out a release saying that you're holding a news conference to announce an important visitor to the parish.

If what you want to convey is not an event but a point of view, maybe your parish's opposition to a hotly contested new zoning ordinance that's going to allow a bar next to your school for the first time, try to get on the editorial page of your daily, neighborhood weekly or diocesan newspaper. A news release for the St. Mary Parent Media Awareness program on media literacy snagged an editorial endorsement in the city's largest newspaper, sparking interest and attendance. An editorial, the official position of the newspaper, carries a lot of weight. But if you can't get that, write your own opinion piece. Depending on length, the newspaper may carry it as a letter to the editor or as what's called an "op-ed piece," which is simply an opinion piece not written by the newspaper. Editorials, letters and op-ed pieces are all among the most widely read features in the newspaper.

For Reflection

- *How can you improve the channels of communication within your parish or ministry setting, especially on controversial issues?*

- *What "good news" activities going on in your ministry right now or happening soon do you consider newsworthy of reporting outside the parish?*

- *Which newspaper or station would be most likely to cover your news? Whom should you contact there to tell (and sell) your story?*

ELEVEN

Spiritual Exercises for a Media Age

Your ministry flows out of and into your spirituality. Each informs the other. So it's appropriate that we close out this book on ministry with a few thoughts on spirituality.

The new culture of the media age cries out for a new spirituality to match. Sometimes that demands taking a counter-cultural approach to the expectations generated by our daily use of the mass media. Other times it means finding spiritual value in those media. As a parish leader you should set the tone for the community by recognizing this in your life as well as talking about it in your ministry.

Spirituality is mostly a matter of internal disposition, but spiritual exercises can help us arrive at that state. We've already looked at some spiritual exercises. The media fast which we discussed in chapter four is a spiritual exercise. So is the process of discernment with which we should be approaching all media productions, reading them with the two lenses of media literacy and the gospel.

Here are some other spiritual exercises for a media age, simple and practical acts to help us keep our spiritual bearings in a multi-media world.

Poverty

The mass media of the United States are commercially sponsored. Their purpose is to sell us things. When the mother in the comic strip "Baby Blues" turns off the television set in one panel, the child Zoe cries in the next "But how am I going to know what I want?" And along with things the media are selling a value system that says, "I am what I own. Buying more will make me better." We need to adopt the spirituality of the Beatitudes, which assure us that material goods don't bring blessings. In fact, the church teaches us that we can never own anything; we can only have stewardship of it. That should be obvious to anyone who has ever had to dispose of the material goods left behind by a parent or other loved one. A richer person may leave more stuff behind—but everyone still has to leave it behind. Responsible stewardship means using goods wisely and sharing them unselfishly.

Spiritual Exercise: Give away something that you *want* but someone else *needs*. Reflect on why you wanted it. Was it heavily advertised in the media? Did you associate it with values blessed by the media rather than the values blessed by Jesus?

Communion

The proliferation of receivers for mass media in American families—multiple televisions, radios and sometimes even computers—has created an atomizing effect. Whereas broadcast media used to pull families together as they watched or listened to programs as a unit, today they often pull families apart as family members scatter to separate programs, separate TVs, separate rooms. In a broader social context as well, media tend to be atomizing and individualizing.

In our family and spiritual lives, we need to recapture the awareness that we are not on this journey alone. We are part of a communion of saints stretching back to the Bible and forward to the end of time. Frequent participation in the Eucharist reminds us of that. So does spending time with canonized saints and other holy ones, companions for the journey who have gone on ahead of us. The Emmaus story is a useful metaphor: The disciples on the road to Emmaus came to know Jesus in the breaking of the bread together. Nourished by the community, we become disciples and apostles. Then when we withdraw from the community to be alone with God it is a retreat to solitude, not separation.

Spiritual Exercise: Like Jesus and his disciples, eat meals with family and friends as often as possible. When you watch television, watch it together in your family. Talk about the values of the program and whether they are the same as or different from the values of Jesus. Discuss interesting Web sites you have found and what you have learned from them.

Pilgrimage

In the electronic media, place is not important. One can be anyplace on TV, the radio or the Internet. If I don't tell you where I am in any of those media, including E-mail, you don't know. But for all the great religious traditions, place is important. Some places are sacred, and journeying there can change you. Going on pilgrimage—a visit to a sacred site for a religious purpose, going beyond the familiar, braving danger and discomfort—is a metaphor for life's journey toward God. That's why the great Catholic social activist Dorothy Day called her column "On Pilgrimage." A virtual pilgrimage isn't the same. Neither is visiting "New York, New York" or "Paris" in Las Vegas.

Spiritual Exercises: Go on pilgrimage to Rome, Jerusalem, Lourdes, Fatima, Assisi or some other sacred site at least once in your life. Go on pilgrimage to a shrine far enough from home to require a journey. Go on pilgrimage to your diocesan Cathedral. Wherever you go, celebrate Eucharist and Reconciliation.

Presence

True presence is necessary in everyday life as well. Since the invention of the telegraph, technology has made it possible for people to communicate instantly over long distances. Today telephones and E-mail connect far-flung friends and family at little or no cost. They keep us "in touch," but they can't let us touch. We are embodied persons, not just minds and souls. We can't hug without being there, and technology will never make that possible. It's important to visit our friends sometimes in person. That's what God did at the Incarnation.

The throngs who flock to see the pope and other great leaders in person, even though the view is probably better on television, bear witness that we human beings crave what psychiatrist Edward M. Hallowell calls "the human moment" that can only happen when two people share the same physical space. But technology makes it possible to avoid that, to sometimes connect with communicating. Even in the era of E-mail, the top of the communications hierarchy is person-to-person contact—in person.

Spiritual Exercise: Visit a friend instead of calling, e-mailing or writing a letter. Make yourself truly present to the other person in all of your daily encounters, whether serious or casual, whether with someone you know or with a stranger.

Icons

We use the word icons in many ways in our image culture. Computer icons are images that we click to access programs. Cultural icons are either living legends who have accomplished so much in their field that they have set the standard or they are celebrities of the moment. Dolls and action figures are icons that teach our children what the ideal man and the ideal woman are supposed to look like, supporting the stereotypes of movies, TV and commercials. Corporate logos, such as those instantly identified all over the world for Nike, Coca-

SPIRITUAL EXERCISES FOR A MEDIA AGE   139

Cola and Disney, are also icons, designed to stimulate positive feelings for the company and the products to which they are attached.

Christians traditionally have had icons, too, especially in the east—painted images of Jesus (God made visible) or Mary and other saints that draw us into the sacred. "What you gaze at you become," iconographer William Hart McNichols, S.J., explained to *America* magazine. We need to rediscover religious icons as spiritual companions, spending some of our time with these saints instead of with celebrities.

Spiritual Exercises: Identify the cultural icons in your home—the images of celebrities or idealized men/women found on refrigerator magnets, T-shirts, posters, collectibles and dolls. Replace them in prominence with one or more religious icons. Spend some time praying with the religious icons. Put a religious icon on your computer wallpaper to remind you what the word "icon" means in the Christian prayer tradition.

Surrender

The struggle to accept the difficulties of life is counter-cultural in the media age. Media are controllable at the touch of a remote control wand or the flick of a pre-set button on a car radio. Many people want and even expect life to be the same way, as depicted in the Garfield cartoon where the lasagna-loving cat stares at a window with a remote in his hand saying "Change! Darn you!" But the deepest religious faith always requires a leap into the mystery, a surrender to that which we can't control. Letting go of those things we hold most dear, including people (see John 20:17) is the way to true serenity. If we pray, or light candles, or go on pilgrimage in an attempt to control God, we should let that go, too.

Spiritual Exercise: Identify the most challenging, painful or hard to accept situation in your life that seems unlikely to

change despite your best human efforts. Pray with Mary
the words of her fiat: "Let it be done to me according to
your word" (Luke 1:38).

Simplicity

There's a big market in simplicity today. You could spend a
lot of money learning how to make your life more simple. To
me, that seems too complicated—and typical of the way we
go about things in our culture. Many of the new technologies
that we have put in charge of our life seem to add complex-
ity and anxiety instead of simplicity. They make it possible to
do more faster, but that isn't always a plus. A family that
accepted a challenge from the *Dayton Daily News* in 2000 to
live a 1950's lifestyle for a week learned that. At the end of
the week, they found themselves reluctant to re-enter life's
high-speed lane and determined to be more selective about
the use of technology. For example, they occasionally turn off
their answering machine now.

I've never owned an answering machine, but for a while
our family had the "Caller ID" feature on our telephone. When
we returned home from being out, I would run to check the
machine and see if anyone called. If no one did, I felt disap-
pointment, whereas formerly I never even wondered if anyone had called. Most of the calls we did receive in our absence
were unimportant. Sometimes when we returned calls our
friends couldn't even remember why they had called. After a
few weeks I realized that this machine was increasing my anxiety level and giving me very little in return. We got rid of
Caller ID and have never missed it.

Spiritual Exercise: Starting on Monday, focus each day for
six days on one of the technologies that you use routinely.
In a typical family that might be cable TV, VCR, cell phone,
computer, answering machine, automated teller machine.
Ask yourself each time you use it whether this technology
makes your life more simple or more complex. Perhaps
keep a journal. On Sunday, reflect on how you might alter

or eliminate your use of each technology to simplify your life.

Time-out

In the world of mass media, everything is urgent. Instant gratification isn't fast enough. So we have news reports while an event is still going on, and reporters fill the airwaves with groundless speculation because no one can wait for the facts. In this the media both reflect and lead a culture of immediacy. We have fast food, fast money, instant pregnancy tests and instant-abortion pills. Time that isn't spent "multi-tasking" is wasted time.

The Church looks at time much differently. The Florida minister who offers a Sunday morning "express service" guaranteed not to last longer than forty-five minutes severely misses the point. Every week God not only offers but commands a day of rest, a day to "waste time" building our relationship with God. Every year the church marks off a season of prayerful preparation for Christmas, while some merchants can't even wait until Halloween to put out the Christmas trees. Buy into church time, not media time.

Spiritual Exercises: Take off your watch on Sunday. Do one thing at a time. Read the newspaper or watch a tape of the evening news a day or two after publication or broadcast; ask yourself whether you really missed anything important.

Peace

The level of violence across all electronic media is high and getting higher. The contradiction to the message of the gospel is explicit in an ad that mocks and inverts the Golden Rule with the message "Do unto your opponents before they do unto you." The ad labels different parts of a Microsoft joy stick according to their functions: "Terrorize," "Humiliate," "Demean." The prevalence of violence in entertainment and in news reportage ("if it bleeds, it leads") has created what some have called "the mean world syndrome," the belief that the world is a lot more violent than it really is. Christians are called to accept the peace of Christ that is beyond all understanding, and go forward in personal peace that is free of unreasoning fear.

Spiritual Exercises: Purge your home of media portraying violence that is gratuitous to the storyline, excessive and unnecessarily explicit in its presentation, and virtually without on-screen consequences in its aftermath. Purge your own language of violent words.

Prayer

The underlying promise of commercials is that if you use this product you won't be lonely (because you'll be forever young, popular, trendy or good-looking) But prayer is the only true answer to loneliness and emptiness. Only God can really fill us up, and prayer is dialogue with God. In her popular book *Amazing Grace*, Kathleen Norris worries that churches which adapt their services to appeal to consumers "blur the lines between entertainment (which is a spectator sport) and worship (which is anything but)." That's the danger of liturgies that become production numbers in an attempt to compete with the spectacle and stimulation of television.

Spiritual Exercises: In this age of interactive media, make your private prayer more interactive by attentive listening for God's response. Make your public prayer in the liturgy more interactive by fully participating instead of treating it as a spectator sport. Reflect your media consumption in your prayer by praying about the news or some other non-fictional television programming that you've watched recently. Use those frustrating moments of waiting to access a computer program or the Internet as occasions for prayer.

TWELVE

Making It Happen

This book has given you a theology and a spirituality for ministry in a media age. It also has provided you with the tools for teaching others to read the signs of the times in mass media and for using the media appropriately in your ministries. Now it's up to you.

Throughout this book I've told you what has worked in other ministry settings. But you have to figure out what will work in yours—how best to incorporate media literacy programs into the parish, for example, and whether to put on a parish film festival in Lent or Advent.

Get input from other members of your ministry team to develop a short-term action plan for the next six months and a long-term action plan for the next three years. Put your plans on paper, but be flexible enough to change the timetable in order to seize opportunities. (The latest rush of merchandising for an over-hyped movie may provide a perfect teaching moment in media literacy, for example.)

Most likely you're going to meet some resistance—and a lot of enthusiasm. Your parishioners know intuitively that mass media are important in their lives and those of their children, perhaps too important.

The majority will welcome learning how to take more control as media consumers who are Christians.

They'll also appreciate your use of media to deliver the gospel message. As for the minority of resisters, your zeal will win them over!

So you have the background, you have the tools, you have (or will have) a plan, you have (or will have) a receptive audience. The only other thing you need is to be Spirit-driven. For that we pray:

> Come, Holy Spirit,
> inspire us
> to read the signs of the times
> in the mass media,
> to recognize those media as powerful gifts of God,
> and to faithfully use them
> to communicate Christ's Gospel
> in our families, in the church and in the world.
> Amen.

Resources

ARTICLES

Waznak, Robert P. "Preaching the Gospel in a Video Culture." In *Media, Culture and Catholicism*, edited by Paul A. Soukup. Kansas City: Sheed & Ward, 1996.

BOOKS

Babin, Pierre, with Mercedes Iannone. *The New Era in Religious Communication.* Translated by David Smith. Minneapolis: Fortress Press, 1991. An important guide to understanding the need for and ways to use media in communicating the faith.

Cormier, Jay. *New Bells for New Steeples: Communicating Strategies for Building Parish Community.* Kansas City: Sheed & Ward, 1990. A convenient handbook.

Fore, William F. *Mythmakers: Gospel, Culture and the Media.* New York: Friendship Press, 1990. Fore draws a sharp contrast between the Gospel of Jesus and the gospel of our media culture, with strong concerns about video violence.

Groothuis, Douglas. *The Soul in Cyberspace.* Grand Rapids, Mich.: Baker Books, 1997. A strong critique of the online culture from an evangelical point of view.

Hereford, Marie Judith, FSP, and Thomas, Corrine, FSP. *A New Babel, A New Pentecost: Communicating the Gospel in a Mass Mediated Culture.* Boston: Pauline Books and Media,

1997. Includes workshop ideas and reproducible handouts for use in a parish or other ministry setting.

Martini, Carlo Maria. *Communicating Christ to the World.* Translated by Thomas M. Lucas, S.J., Kansas City: Sheed & Ward, 1994. Perceptive spiritual treatment of the relationship between church and media.

McKibben, Bill. *The Age of Missing Information.* New York: Random House, 1992. The author finds that he learns more from a day in the woods than from watching a hundred hours of cable TV.

Meyrowitz, Joshua. *No Sense of Place: The Impact of Electronic Media on Social Behavior.* New York: Oxford University, 1985. A groundbreaking work examining the sociological effects of electronic media, particularly television.

Niebuhr, H. Richard. *Christ and Culture.* New York: Harper & Brothers, 1951. The classic book exploring the various possible relationships between Christians and culture.

Postman, Neil. *Amusing Ourselves to Death: Public Discourse in the Age of Show Business.* New York: Penguin Books, 1985. Seminal critique of the entertainment culture.

———. *Technopoly: The Surrender of Culture to Technology.* New York: Vintage Books, 1993. Poses important questions about technology.

Riley, Fr. Miles O'Brien. *Tell the Truth...With Kindness.* Orinda, Ca.: Perfect Page Publishing, 1999. Ten essentials for effective communication by a veteran Catholic communicator. Great tips for dealing with TV and other news media. Workbook format.

Sarno, Ronald A. *Using Media in Religious Education.* Birmingham, Ala.: Religious Education Press, 1987. About half of the book painstakingly builds the case for using media in religious education and half offers exercises and resources.

Schultze, Quentin J. *Internet for Christians: Everything You Need to Start Cruising the Net Today.* Muskegon, Mich:

Gospel Films Publications, 1996. An excellent starter kit
for beginners in clear language, with a 72-page appendix
of resources on the Net that is also available in
cyberspace.

Silverblatt, Art. *Media Literacy: Keys to Interpreting Media
Messages*. Westport, Conn.: Praeger Publishers, 1995. An
excellent textbook.

Stauffer, Dennis. *MEDIASMART: How to Handle a Reporter, By
a Reporter*. Minneapolis: MinneApplePress, 1994. Good
guide to all aspects of press relations.

Trampiets, Fran, S.C. *Faith in the Media?* Notre Dame, Ind.:
Ave Maria Press, 1997. An excellent mini-course for
teens.

Troeger, Thomas H. *Ten Strategies for Preaching in a
MultiMedia Culture*. Nashville: Abingdon Press, 1996.
Opens up some creative possibilities.

Untener, Ken. *Preaching Better: Practical Suggestions for
Homilists*. New York: Paulist Press, 1999.

Walsh, David, Ph.D. *Selling Out America's Children: How
America Puts Profits Before Values—and What Parents Can
Do*. Minneapolis: Fairview Press, 1994. Largely a critique
of TV and advertising for promoting bad values, with
many concrete suggestions for family solutions.

Webster, Douglas D. *Selling Jesus: What's Wrong With
Marketing the Church*. Downer's Grove, Ill.: InterVarsity
Press, 1992. A strong critique of the church growth
movement and the way it mirrors the mass-mediated
culture.

Zaleski, Jeff. *The Soul of Cyberspace: How New Technology is
Changing Our Spiritual Lives*. San Francisco: HarperEdge,
1997. A series of interviews with both religious and
computer gurus who offer sometimes-conflicting
viewpoints on spirituality and cyberspace.

(Several guides to Christian Web sites are available, but it
seems unproductive to list books that so quickly become
outdated.)

BOOKLETS

National Conference of Catholic Bishops / United States
Catholic Conference. *Renewing the Mind of the Media*, a 40-
page statement from the U.S. bishops in 1998 intended as
a starting point for dioceses, parishes, and others to
reflect on exploitative sex and gratuitous violence in the
mass media. Order from the NCCB/USCC at (800) 235-
8722.

Pacatte, Sr. Rose. *Guide to Planning In-House Film Festivals: A
Media Education Opportunity in Ten Easy Steps.* Pauline
Center for Media Studies, 50 Saint Pauls Avenue, Boston,
MA 02130-3491, (617) 522-8911, FAX (617) 524-8648.
More details on how to put together a film festival for
any group. *more than what?*

Sterner, Sr. Matthias, OP, and Zukowski, Sr. Angela Ann,
MHSH. *Designing a Parish Media Resource Center.* Center
for Pastoral Initiatives (formerly the Center for Religious
Telecommunications), University of Dayton, 300 College
Park, Dayton, OH 45469-0314.

*Taking Charge of Your TV: A Guide to Critical Viewing for Parents
and Children*, a practical 18-page manual sponsored by
the Family & Critical Viewing Project of the National
Parent Teacher Association, the National Cable Television
Association and Cable in the Classroom. Companion to
the video of the same name. Free by calling (800) 743-
5355.

BROCHURE

"Family Guide for Using Media," an eight-panel brochure
from the National Conference of Catholic
Bishops/United States Catholic Conference identifying
ten actions or attitudes to affirm Christian values in
evaluating or using media. Order from the NCCB/
USCC at (800) 235-8722.

CHURCH DOCUMENT

Fulfilled in Your Hearing: The Homily in the Sunday Assembly.
National Conference of Catholic Bishops / United States
Catholic Conference, 1982. Order from the NCCB/USSC
at (800) 235-8722.

JOURNALS

REEL TO REAL: Making the Most of the Movies with Youth.
Abingdon Press, P.O. Box 801, 201 Eighth Avenue, South,
Nashville, TN. 37202-0801, (800) 672-1789. The subtitle
says it all. A great resource for youth ministry.

Visual Parables: A Christian Film & Video Guide. P.O. Box 58,
Topeka, KS 66601-0058, (800) 528-6522. A monthly aid to
finding the sacred in celluloid. Includes "Lectionary
Links" suggesting film connections to the common
lectionary.

PASTORAL LETTER

Mahony, Cardinal Roger. "Film Makers, Film Viewers: Their
Challenges and Opportunities." A wonderful reflection
tool for study groups. On the Internet at
http://cardinal.la-archdiocese.org/920915.html and in
print from St. Paul Books & Media.

VIDEOS

Advertising Consciousness and Culture: The Depersonalization of
American Life. With Rev. John F. Kavanaugh, S.J. Loyola
Tapes, Sacred Heart Program, 3900 Westminister, St.
Louis, MO 63108-3191; (888) 7-CONTACT.

Catholic Connections to Media Literacy. A kit including video
and books with lesson plans, handouts. Center for Media
Literacy, 4727 Wilshire Blvd., Suite 403, Los Angeles, CA
90010; (800) 226-9494, FAX (213) 931-4474.

Renewing the Mind of the Media, a 12-minute video prepared
by the U.S. bishops' Committee on Communications in
1999 as a companion to the print document of the same
name. Order from the NCCB/USCC at (800) 235-8722.

Signs of the Times: Reading Our Culture with the Eyes of Faith
(an eight-part series), CTS Press, P.O. Box 520, Decatur,
GA 30031; (404) 289-8952. Looks at television and the
computer as well as some non-electronic signs of the
times.

Taking Charge of Your TV. A four-minute video with Rosie
O'Donnell. Available from the Family and Community
Critical Viewing Project, 1724 Massachusetts Avenue,
NW, Washington, DC 20036, (202) 775-1044.

WEB SITES

Adbusters (www.adbusters.org), the organization that calls
attention to the commercial culture by creating spoof ads
and promoting the day after Thanksgiving as "Buy
Nothing Day."

The American Psychological Association
(www.apa.org/pubinfo/violence.html), summarizes
research findings that violent programs on television can
lead to aggressive behavior in children and adolescents
and suggests what parents can do about it.

Center for Media Literacy (www.medialit.org), the leading
U.S. media literacy organization; it sponsors workshops,
creates and sells media literacy materials. This site's
"Reading Room" includes a core resource checklist for a
media literacy program in Catholic schools and parishes.

Evangelism: Guide to Internet Web Outreach
(www.gospelcom.net/guide/web-
evangelism.html#web?ifc), an exhaustive online guide to
evangelism via the Internet, crammed with advice and
links.

Go Tell Communications (www.gotell.org), an ecumenical, not-for-profit ministry devoted to empowering the Church in an electronic culture.

God Speaks (www.godspeaks.net), the Web page for a group that produced a series of well known billboards bearing messages from God.

The Gospel and Our Culture Network (www.gocn.org), a network for encouraging the encounter between Gospel and culture in North America.

Heidi A. Campbell (www.ed.ac.uk/~ewcv24/index.htm), a Ph.D. candidate at the University of Edinburgh (Scotland) who is researching religious online communities.

The Henry J. Kaiser Family Foundation (www.kff.org), includes the text of the "Kids & Media @The New Millennium" report.

Hollywood Jesus (www.hollywoodjesus.com), exploring pop culture (specifically, the movies) from a religious point of view.

The Institute for Pastoral Initiatives (www.udayton.edu./~ipi) at the University of Dayton, strongly involved with media literacy from a Christian perspective.

Jesuit Communications Project (http://interact.uoregon.edu/MediaLit/JCP), Web site for a Roman Catholic (but not always explicitly religious) organization that works to encourage, promote, and develop media education in schools across Canada.

JM Communications (www.jmcommunications.com), an eclectic media and religious site that includes the home page for the International Study Commission on Media, Religion and Culture.

Just Think Foundation (www.justthink.org), created to help young people understand media, includes lesson plans for teachers on this Web page.

✦ Media Literacy Online Project
      (http://interact.uoregon.edu/MediaLit/HomePage), a
      comprehensive guide to online media literacy resources.

National Institute on Media and the Family
      (www.mediafamily.org), an organization formed "to
      maximize the benefits and minimize the harm of media
      on children and families through research and
      education."

The New Media Bible (www.newmediabible.org), a project of
      the American Bible Society's Research Center for Bible
      and Media (www.researchcenter.org), presents Scripture
      multimedia formats, including samples from a CD.

NewTech '98 (www.newtech.org), the official Web site of the
      International Conference on New Technologies and the
      Human Person, which took place in Denver in March
      1998 under Catholic Church sponsorship.

Pauline Books & Media (www.pauline.org), operated by the
      Daughters of St. Paul, includes "Resources on Social
      Communications" in its online catalog. Also within this
      site the Pauline Center for Media Studies
      (www.pauline.org/mediastudies/index.html) gives
      online access to articles about media literacy, often from a
      faith perspective.

Religion Online (www.religion-online.org), William Fore's
      site offering full texts for religious seekers and scholars,
      including sections on Religions and Communications,
      Media Education and Religion and Culture.

Religious Education and the Challenge of Media Culture,
      (www.bc.edu/bc_org/avp/acavp/irepm/challenge/mrc
      source.html), a group of thinkers from both academic
      and religious institutions who have joined to explore the
      latest research on the convergence of media, religion and
      culture for its implications for religious education.

Symbolism, Media and the Lifecourse project at the
University of Colorado
(www.colorado.edu/Journalism/MEDIALYF), exploring
the religion of the media age.

TV Free America (www.tvfa.org), the organization that
supports the annual National TV Turnoff Week, includes
persuasive statistics, essays and testimonials on this Web
site, but not from a spiritual perspective. It posts articles
of interest even for those who want to manage TV rather
than eliminate it from their lives.

The Un-TV Guide (www.sover.net/~gmws/untv) from the
Green Mountain Waldorf School, includes research
summaries on the effects of television viewing and tips
on how to tell if your children are watching too much
television. It also supports National TV Turnoff Week.

WebChurch — Scotland's Virtual Church
(www.webchurch.org/in), a particularly interesting
religious Web site with an emphasis on spirituality and
side chapels (links) for particular religious traditions.